The
Grapes of Wrath
Trouble in the Promised Land

TWAYNE'S MASTERWORK STUDIES
Robert Lecker, General Editor

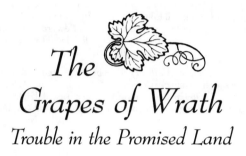

The Grapes of Wrath
Trouble in the Promised Land

LOUIS OWENS

TWAYNE PUBLISHERS

NEW YORK

Twayne's Masterwork Studies No. 27

Copyright 1996 Simon & Schuster Macmillan
All rights reserved.
Twayne Publishers

1633 Broadway
New York, NY 10019-6785

Printed on permanent/durable acid-free paper
and bound in the United States of America.

Library of Congress Cataloging-in-Publication Data

Owens, Louis.
    The grapes of wrath : trouble in the promised land / Louis Owens.
        p.   cm. — (Twayne's masterwork studies ; no. 27)
    Bibliography: p.
    Includes index.
    ISBN 0-8057-7998-1. — ISBN 0-8057-8047-5 (pbk.)
    1. Steinbeck, John, 1902-1968.   Grapes of wrath.   I. Title.
II. Series.
PS3537.T3234G88   1989
813'.52—dc19   88-37315
                                                          CIP

12   11   10   9   8   7

For Jim and Roberta

CONTENTS

The new eye is being opened here in the west —
the new seeing.

—John Steinbeck

NOTE ON THE REFERENCES AND ACKNOWLEDGMENTS

For this study I have relied upon Penguin Books' paperback edition of *The Grapes of Wrath,* an edition readily available to most readers. Page references are to this edition and are provided parenthetically within the text of my discussion. I have also relied upon the outstanding work of the many Steinbeck critics who have preceded me, scholars such as Warren French, Peter Lisca, Joseph Fontenrose, John Ditsky, Richard Astro, Robert DeMott, Clifford Lewis, Mimi Reisel Gladstein, and others too numerous to name. I owe much to the graduate and undergraduate students both in the United States and Europe who have helped me over the last few years to come to terms with this novel.

I would like to thank the staff of the John Steinbeck Research Center for their assistance in my work on this and other Steinbeck studies and the University of New Mexico Research Allocations Committee for the grants which made this work possible. Finally I, like all those with an interest in Steinbeck's writing, owe an enormous debt to Tetsumaro Hayashi for his years of invaluable labor in creating and sustaining the International Steinbeck Society and the *Steinbeck Quarterly,* as well as for his hard work in the furthering of Steinbeck scholarship.

John Steinbeck receiving the Nobel Prize for Literature in 1962. Courtesy of the Steinbeck Research Center, San Jose State University Library, San Jose, California.

CHRONOLOGY: JOHN STEINBECK'S LIFE AND WORKS

1902   John Ernst Steinbeck born 27 February in Salinas, California to John Ernst Steinbeck ("senior" and "junior" were not used), treasurer of Monterey County, California, and Olive Hamilton Steinbeck, until her marriage a small-town schoolteacher.

1919   John Steinbeck graduates from Salinas High School, having edited the class yearbook but is otherwise undistinguished, either academically or athletically, among a class of twenty-four. In the fall he enrolls at Stanford University to begin a sporadic and equally undistinguished college career that ends six years later with no degree.

1920   Steinbeck drops out of Stanford in the first of many withdrawals to work as "straw boss" on a Spreckles ranch ten miles south of Salinas, experience that later bears fruit in the novella *Of Mice and Men*.

1922   Works nights as supervisory "bench chemist" at the Spreckles sugar refinery near Salinas, gathering stories that play a large part in the makeup of *Tortilla Flat*.

1923   Steinbeck and his sister Mary enroll for summer quarter at Hopkins Marine Station in Pacific Grove, near Monterey, the beginning of Steinbeck's lifelong fascination with marine biology.

1924   Steinbeck stories appear in the Stanford *Spectator*.

1925   Drops out of Stanford for good and takes a summer position as handyman at a Fallen Leaf Lake resort near Lake Tahoe. In November he goes to Los Angeles where he boards a freighter for New York to make his name as a writer. Passage through the Panama Canal plants the seeds of Steinbeck's first novel, *Cup of Gold*, a fictionalized account of the pirate Henry Morgan. Jobs in New York as cub newspaper reporter and hod carrier leave him broke and unpublished.

1926   Works his way home to California on a freighter and returns to Fallen Leaf Lake. Employed for the winter as caretaker at a private lodge, begins *Cup of Gold,* allowing snow to pile up and crush the lodge's roof as he writes. Meets Carol Henning, whom he convinces to type his manuscript.

1929   *Cup of Gold,* after many revisions, is published with swashbuckling cover mistakenly aimed at adolescents. The novel does not sell.

1930   Steinbeck marries Carol Henning and moves to parents' summer cottage in Pacific Grove with $25 a month stipend from father. Works on second novel, *To a God Unknown,* begun at Fallen Leaf Lake. Meets Edward Ricketts, the marine biologist who becomes a lifelong friend, mentor, and model for the "Doc" character in "The Snake," *Cannery Row, Sweet Thursday,* and *In Dubious Battle.* Writes stories making up *Pastures of Heaven* while failing to find publisher for *To a God Unknown.*

1932   *Pastures of Heaven* published to poor sales. Revises *To a God Unknown* and moves for a short time to Los Angeles.

1933   Returns to Pacific Grove. *To a God Unknown* published and sells dismally. Illness of mother, Olive Steinbeck. Sits at her bedside, writing stories that will make up *The Red Pony,* the first two parts of which appear in the *North American Review.*

1934   Steinbeck's mother dies. His story "The Murder" is included in the *O. Henry Prize Stories* for that year.

1935   *Tortilla Flat* published. Written during a time of personal tragedy, it is the most comic of Steinbeck's novels. The novel wins the California Commonwealth Club Gold Medal, and for the first time a Steinbeck work sells well. His years of poverty are over. Meanwhile, he is researching the farm labor novel, *In Dubious Battle,* interviewing radical union organizers.

1936   *In Dubious Battle* published while Steinbeck works on his first play-novella, *Of Mice and Men. In Dubious Battle* raises controversy about the author's supposed Marxism, sells moderately well. Steinbeck and Carol move to Los Gatos. Father dies. Steinbeck researches and writes "The Harvest Gypsies," eight articles for the *San Francisco News* that are the beginning of his fascination with and concern for the plight of migrant farm workers in the Central Valley.

1937   *Of Mice and Men* published, the author's first best-seller. Stage version, produced by George Kaufman, wins the prestigious Drama Critics' Circle Award in New York. Steinbeck travels to Europe for the first time, beginning a long fascination with Europe. *Time* magazine publishes essay-review panning the author and complaining about "Steinbeck Inflation."

1938   Steinbeck finishes draft of *The Grapes of Wrath*, titled at this time "L'Affaire Lettuceberg." After a week of consideration, he burns the draft and begins again. Completes new draft in December. Carol names it *The Grapes of Wrath*. Steinbeck's only collection of short fiction, *The Long Valley*, is published. *Their Blood Is Strong*, collected essays from "The Harvest Gypsies" plus an epilogue, is published.

1939   *The Grapes of Wrath* published and is a best-seller. Darryl F. Zanuck buys rights to the novel and sends detectives to the Central Valley to check authenticity before beginning filming. Steinbeck is denounced in Congress for his radical novel.

1940   *Grapes of Wrath* wins Pulitzer Prize. Steinbeck makes collecting trip to Gulf of California with Ed Ricketts. Writes and works on filming of documentary, *The Forgotten Village*, in Mexico.

1941   *Sea of Cortez: A Leisurely Journey of Travel and Research*, from Steinbeck's and Ricketts's journals during Gulf of California trip, is published. *The Forgotten Village* published in book form. *Of Mice and Men* and *The Grapes of Wrath* films released.

1942   Propaganda piece, *Bombs Away: The Story of a Bomber Team*, written and published for the Army Air Corps. Second play-novella, *The Moon Is Down*, published. The story of totalitarian occupation of a small European country, written while Steinbeck was on assignment for what becomes the Central Intelligence Agency, *The Moon is Down* becomes immensely popular in northern Europe and is circulated underground in Nazi-occupied countries. Steinbeck is divorced from Carol Henning.

1943   Marries Gwyndolen Conger and applies for security clearances from War and State Departments in order to cover the war in Europe. Despite being secretly labeled a Communist sympathizer by the American Legion Radical Research Bureau, he is eventually allowed to leave Gwyn in New York and sail for England and North Africa as a reporter for the New York *Herald Tribune*. Returns from war after several months and establishes residence in New York. Works on scripts for the Hitchcock movie *Lifeboat* and, with Jack Wagner, the propaganda film *A Medal for Benny*.

1944   Son Thom born. The movie *Lifeboat* is released. Disapproving of Hitchcock's direction and what he feels to be the film's racism, Steinbeck demands his name be removed from list of credits for the film.

1945   *Cannery Row* published. *The Red Pony* published in four parts. *The Pearl* appears in *Woman's Home Companion* under title of "The Pearl of the World."

1946   Second son, John IV, born.

1947   *The Wayward Bus* published. *The Pearl* published in novel form. Steinbeck travels to Russia with photographer Robert Capa.

1948   *A Russian Journal*, Steinbeck's writing and Capa's photographs, published. Divorced from Gwyn Conger. Edward F. Ricketts, Steinbeck's closest friend, is killed in auto accident. The author is elected to the American Academy of Arts and Letters.

1949   Film version of *The Red Pony* released. Steinbeck works on script for Darryl F. Zanuck movie *Viva Zapata!*

1950   *Viva Zapata!* released. *Burning Bright*, another experimental play-novella, published. Marries Elaine Scott, ex-wife of actor Zachary Scott.

1951   *The Log from the Sea of Cortez*, with Steinbeck's preface, "About Ed Ricketts," published.

1952   *East of Eden* published, the novel Steinbeck considered his most difficult and most important. On assignment for *Colliers*, Steinbeck and his new wife travel to Europe. Steinbeck is attacked in print by editor of *L'Unità*, Italy's largest left-wing newspaper. Steinbeck replies in Italian newspapers, creating a minor political sensation.

1954   *Sweet Thursday*, a quasi-sequel to *Cannery Row*, published. Steinbecks spend nine months in Europe, where Steinbeck writes for *Figaro* in Paris and begins *The Short Reign of Pippin IV*, a novella set in Paris.

1955   *Pipe Dream*, the musical comedy version of *Sweet Thursday*, adapted by Richard Rogers and Oscar Hammerstein, produced in New York. Play is a flop. Steinbeck buys house in Sag Harbor, Long Island.

1957   *The Short Reign of Pippin IV: A Fabrication* is published with little enthusiasm by Steinbeck's editors at Viking Press. Travels to Europe and begins serious research into Malory in preparation for his "translation" of *Morte d'Arthur*.

1958   *Once There Was a War,* collection of dispatches written during World War II, is published, displaying Steinbeck's ingenious use of Jungian archetypes to unify disparate materials. Returns to England for Malory research.

1959   Spends almost a full year at Discove Cottage in England working on his version of *Morte d'Arthur.* Battles English weather to plant a garden and declares himself gloriously happy.

1960   Returns to United States to work on *Morte.* Puts Malory on hold in order to rediscover America on cross-country journey that will lead to *Travels with Charley.*

1961   *The Winter of Our Discontent,* Steinbeck's indictment of the American conscience and his final novel, published. Travels to Europe with Elaine and both sons.

1962   Returns to United States in early summer. *Travels with Charley in Search of America* published. He turns on the television one morning to learn that he has been awarded the Nobel Prize for Literature.

1963   Travels to Eastern Europe with playwright Edward Albee on cultural exchange. Is asked in Berlin why he had "turned from being a Marxist to a puritan." Steinbeck replies, "I've never been either. My novels of social reform were stories of people, not political treatises."

1964   Is awarded the Presidential Medal of Freedom by President Lyndon Johnson. Pascal Covici, Steinbeck's lifelong friend and editor, dies. Steinbecks travel to Ireland for Christmas.

1965   Travels to Europe and London. Sister Mary Dekker dies. Spends Christmas in Ireland.

1966   Travels to Israel on assignment for *Newsday.* Publishes *America and Americans,* still another study of his homeland. Travels to Southeast Asia for *Newsday* as war in Vietnam is heating up.

1968   Suffers heart attack at Sag Harbor in May, a second attack in New York in July. Dies 20 December in New York City, a continent away from the place of his birth and the settings of his greatest fiction.

1969   The *East of Eden* letters, written to Pascal Covici as Steinbeck worked on his longest novel, are published as *Journal of a Novel.*

1975   *The Acts of King Arthur and His Noble Knights,* the unfinished draft of Steinbeck's version of *Morte d'Arthur,* is published.

Migrants line up for state relief checks at barn used for Workers' Alliance meetings, church services, and check distribution. Courtesy of the Steinbeck Research Center, San Jose State University Library, San Jose, California.

1

Historical Context

Two great historical and social phenomena converged in the thirties to make *The Grapes of Wrath* possible for John Steinbeck. The first of these was a new class consciousness that had been growing in America since the turn of the century, with a pronounced interest by American intellectuals in Marxism, socialism, or communism, as a means of helping the oppressed worker. The second, and for Steinbeck by far the more important phenomenon, was the ecological terror that blew across fifty million acres of the Midwest and Southwest in the form of the Dust Bowl, which eventually sent between three and four hundred thousand Americans in search of new lives in California where the dust never blew.

By the end of the nineteenth century America had become a world industrial power and, with the advent of the Spanish American War and with World War II to follow, America was to become a preeminent world military power. America was flexing its economic and military muscles around the globe. At home, however, a new awareness of the human cost of such growth was entering our literature. Stephen Crane, in *Maggie, A Girl of the Streets*, Upton Sinclair, in *The Jungle*, and Frank Norris, in *The Octopus*, were illustrating the tragic waste of lives in the urban slums, packing houses, and wheat fields. Attempts by workers to organize for better conditions and pay in the mining camps of the Rockies and the logging camps of the Northwest were effectively crushed in bloody confrontations between workers and management.

In the thirties, labor agitation in the West shifted from the mining and logging camps to the fields of California. In November 1933 a gigantic dust cloud rose over an area of the United States stretching from Texas to South Dakota; it was a presage of the horror in store for midwestern and southwestern farmers. As the drought worsened, the topsoil of this region was lifted and blown away by the constant winds. Crop after crop failed, and small farmers lost their land to the banks that held mortgages on their farms. Corporations were formed to farm the land under more intensive wide-scale operations. Tractors replaced the small farmers' horse-drawn plows. Like the Joads, thousands of small farmers and sharecroppers were evicted from the land their parents and grandparents had settled. Left with no alternative, the new migrants invested what was left in rattletrap cars and trucks and set out for the promise of California. Their influx would eventually more than double the state's average population of 200,000 farm laborers and create desperate competition for what little work there was.

In 1934 John Steinbeck was living with his first wife, Carol Henning, in Pacific Grove, a small community adjoining Monterey. He had published three novels whose themes were far removed from the immediate plight of workers—*Cup of Gold, The Pastures of Heaven,* and *To a God Unknown*—and was about to publish a fourth, the humorous *Tortilla Flat.* He was penniless and complained in a letter, "Still we have no money. I've sent off story after story and so far with no result."[1] Meanwhile, Steinbeck's hometown of Salinas, twenty-five miles to the east of Monterey, was becoming a center for the growing violence between corporate agriculture and migrant laborers. With conditions in the fields and labor camps intolerable, thousands of workers suffering from disease and starvation, and hourly wages as low as twelve-and-a-half cents, Communist party workers had come to the state in order to help the field workers to organize. The result was the Cannery & Agricultural Workers' Industrial Union (C&AWIU). Having discovered that two of the C&AWIU organizers were in hiding nearby, Steinbeck arranged to interview the pair. Though he never wrote the biographical story he had in mind, this meeting began a process of education for Steinbeck that would culminate in the short stories entitled "The Vigilante" and "The Raid," as well as Steinbeck's greatest novels, *In Dubious Battle, Of Mice and Men,* and *The Grapes of Wrath.* While, contrary to widespread opinion, Steinbeck was never sympathetic to communism, the author's sympathies would from this time forward lie more and more with the oppressed migrant laborer, and his lifelong loathing of middle-class materialism would evolve into a powerful resentment of corporate agriculture in California.

By 1936 Steinbeck had written a brief description of the plight of the migrants for the *Nation* and he had published *In Dubious Battle,* a novel that takes a hard look at the tactics of communist strike organizers as well as the oppressive land owners. In this novel, however, the author's interest lay not in helping the downtrodden worker, but in the abstract concept of what Steinbeck called "group man." "I'm not interested in [the] strike as a means of raising men's wages," he wrote at the time, "and I'm not interested in ranting about justice and oppression, mere outcroppings which indicate the conditions."[2] During the same year that *In Dubious Battle* was published, however, Steinbeck's sympathies were becoming sharpened. "There are riots in Salinas and killings in the streets of that dear little town where I was born," he wrote to a friend.[3] When *Life* magazine asked him to report on migrant conditions in California in 1936, he refused on the grounds that it would be immoral to make money from the plight of the workers. He did, however, agree to do a series of articles for the *San Francisco News.* Published between 5 October and 12 October 1936 and subsequently collected in a pamphlet entitled *Their Blood Is Strong,* Steinbeck's essays are firsthand accounts of the grim picture of starving children, disease, and filth in the migrants' camps across the state, a picture much more brutal than anything he would later evoke in *The Grapes of Wrath.*

Conditions for the migrants in California continued to worsen during the latter half of the thirties. In 1937 seventy thousand workers flooded into the San Joaquin Valley for the harvest of the cotton crop. In his book documenting farm-labor conditions in California, *Factories in the Fields*, Carey McWilliams wrote,"Lured to the valley by announcements that 25,000 additional workers were required to harvest the 1937 cotton crop, a vast army of transients had assembled there to starve."[4] McWilliams cites an observer for the Gospel Army who declared at this time that "people are seeking shelter and subsistence in the fields and woods like wild animals, and that children were working in the cotton fields for 15 and 20 cents a day."[5] The population of Madera County in central California nearly doubled with the influx of migrants. With conditions for workers worsening, strikes began to break out from one end of California to the other, with 180 strikes occurring between 1933 and 1939, the year *The Grapes of Wrath* appeared.

As more and more of the displaced residents of Oklahoma, Arkansas, Texas, and other Dust Bowl states moved west, California's citizens became anxious. One health official, in a 1938 speech to the Junior Lions Club of Fresno, in California's Central Valley, described the migrants as "incapable of being absorbed into our civilization," and declared that "You cannot legislate these people out of California. . . but you can make it difficult for them when they are here."[6] To make it difficult for the migrants to settle in particular parts of the state, California communities deputized hundreds of citizens. The umbrella organization for organized agricultural interests, the Associated Farmers, prepared plans for a citizens' army of six hundred men to control striking workers. When workers organized a strike meeting in a public park in Madera on 21 October 1939, six hundred men wearing Associated Farmers arm bands, under the scrutiny of Madera Sheriff W. O. Justice, attacked the gathering, and injured scores of participants and bystanders including a congressional investigator.

Visiting the labor camps for his newspaper articles, Steinbeck quickly saw how difficult life was for the migrants. Writing to his agent, Elizabeth Otis, early in 1938, he said, "I must go over to the interior valleys. There are about five thousand families starving to death over there, not just hungry but actually starving. The government is trying to feed them and get medical attention to them with the fascist group of utilities and banks and huge growers sabotaging the thing all along the line. . . . I've tied into the thing from the first and I must get down there and see it and see if I can't do something to help knock these murderers on the heads. . . . I'm pretty mad about it."[7] He decided to write a "big book" exposing the depth of the suffering and oppression, declaring in the same letter to Elizabeth Otis, "Funny how mean and little books become in the face of such tragedies."[8] In preparation for this big book, Steinbeck teamed up with government labor camp manager Tom Collins (to whom *The Grapes of Wrath* is dedicated) and the two men worked their way down much of the length of California as farm laborers. Collins, manager of the first of fifteen government camps set up for migrants in California, became the model for the heroic camp manager in *The Grapes of Wrath* as well as Steinbeck's source for much information in the novel.

By 1942, in an essay entitled "California Pastoral," Carey McWilliams laid to rest all charges of inaccuracy in *The Grapes of Wrath*, marshalling overwhelming evidence of the novel's honesty in depicting the conditions in California's fields during the thirties. Federal hearings had been held in San Francisco beginning in December 1939, during which time, McWilliams states, "John Steinbeck was warmly denounced as the archenemy, defamer, and slanderer of migratory farm labor in California, while I was tenderly referred to as 'Agricultural Pest No.1 in California, outranking pear blight and boll weevil.' "[9] The Dust Bowl and the ensuing flood of displaced "Okies," the national economic depression of the thirties, and the growing plight of the oppressed worker all converged in the thirties to powerfully affect the direction of Steinbeck's thought and art. For a brief time, a period of no more than half a decade, he would become a political writer, painting the suffering of the worker in capitalist society more effectively than any American writer before or since.

Federal government Wheat Patch Camp, the model for "Weedpatch" camp in *The Grapes of Wrath*. Courtesy of the Steinbeck Research Center, San Jose State University Library, San Jose, California.

2

The Importance of the Work

The 1930s in America was the great decade of the "proletarian" novel, which sought explicitly to document the oppression of the downtrodden masses. During this decade writers flirted heavily with the Communist party and wrote fiction for the proletariat. Henry Roth, John Dos Passos, James T. Farrell, Tillie Olson, Daniel Fuchs, Robert Cantwell, James Agee, Edmund Wilson, Josephine Herbst, and many other writers sympathetic to leftist causes and, more particularly, to the working masses published important books during this time. None, however, achieved the enormous popular success of John Steinbeck's *The Grapes of Wrath*. No novel since Harriet Beecher Stowe's *Uncle Tom's Cabin*, in fact, has had the combined popularity and social impact of *The Grapes of Wrath*, a novel that sold more than 400,000 copies during its first year in print.

We can and should read *The Grapes of Wrath* as a testament to a historical and sociological phenomenon—the Dust Bowl—perhaps the greatest combined ecological and social catastrophe in American history. In a letter to his agents, Steinbeck declared, "I am trying to write history while it is happening and I don't want to be wrong."[10] In his attempt to "write history while it is happening," Steinbeck brilliantly documents the suffering of a people in flight, the tragic loss of homeland, and the discovery that in the land of plenty there isn't enough to go around. Simultaneously, *The Grapes of Wrath* offers an education in the dynamics of the laboring class. Unlike the ruthlessly microscopic perspective of *In Dubious Battle,* Steinbeck's previous strike novel, *The Grapes of Wrath* demonstrates how labor organizations, or unions, grow from the desperation of the workers, how capitalism, in its inherent quest for the profit that keeps the machinery going, will oppress and even destroy the laborer. The novel serves as a powerful reminder of the struggle to organize the working class during the twenties and thirties as well as a reminder of the widespread fears of communism that lasted through the McCarthy era of the fifties.

These are historical and political reasons to read this novel, but no great novel can or should be read merely for such reasons. *The Grapes of Wrath* endures. It is taught in high schools and colleges and at the same time it is read throughout the world by men and women with little education. In this book Steinbeck brings together vital threads central to American thought, American history, and American letters. Behind the political and historical message lies the archetypal pattern of American consciousness, the so-called American myth. Behind the preacher Casy's eloquence lies Emersonian transcendentalism as well as Steinbeck's interest in biology and ecology. Behind the hunger for the land expressed in both the narrator's and the characters' words lies Jeffersonian agrarianism, a quintessential element in the American Dream, but a Jeffersonian agrarianism that is questioned and revised in the course of the novel. Behind the exodus from the Dust Bowl to the Eden of California lies the inevitable human need to believe in a new beginning, a second chance, the possibility of Eden rediscovered.

And containing all of these streams of thought is a superbly crafted work of fiction, a novel that takes impressive risks and succeeds. In this novel Steinbeck's mastery of a complex array of prose styles is apparent, as is his ability to engage the reader's sympathies for characters while consistently undercutting the tendencies toward sentimentality in the creation of such characters.

The Importance of the Work

In American literature only one novel had previously brought together the political, sociological, and aesthetic power found in *The Grapes of Wrath*: Mark Twain's *Adventures of Huckleberry Finn*, with its searing indictment of the South, of the institution of slavery, and of the human conscience, and its unequalled brilliance in the use of a vernacular narrator.

3

Critical Reception

"Literary criticism," John Steinbeck declared in "A Letter on Criticism," "is a kind of ill tempered parlour game in which nobody gets kissed." Steinbeck went on to write, "I don't think the *Grapes of Wrath* [sic] is obscure in what it tries to say. As to its classification and pickling, I have neither opinion nor interest. It's just a book, interesting I hope, instructive in the same way the writing instructed me. Its structure is very carefully worked out and it is no more intended to be inspected than is the skeletal structure of a pretty girl. Just read it, don't count it!"[11]

The structure was indeed carefully worked out. Steinbeck had burned an early completed draft of the novel, tentatively entitled "L'Affaire Lettuceberg," because he was not satisfied with it. He wrote to his publisher, Pascal Covici, "You see this book is finished and it is a bad book and I must get rid of it. It can't be printed. It is bad because it isn't honest. . . . My whole work drive has been aimed at making people understand each other and then I deliberately write this book, the aim of which is to cause hatred through partial understanding. . . . If I can't do better I have slipped badly. And that I won't admit—yet."[12]

Steinbeck began again, and finally completed the novel we know as *The Grapes of Wrath*. Refusing to bow to requests that he change the novel's abrupt and disturbing conclusion, in which Rose of Sharon gives her breast to a dying man, Steinbeck wrote to Covici: "I know that books lead to a strong climax. This one doesn't except by implication and the reader must bring the implication to it. If he doesn't, it wasn't a book for him to read. Throughout I've tried to make the reader participate in the actuality, what he takes from it will be scaled entirely on his own depth or hollowness. There are five layers in this book; a reader will find as many as he can and he won't find more than he has in himself."[13]

If criticism is a parlor game, to observe the critical history of *The Grapes of Wrath* is to observe an enormously popular work that has only gradually come to be accepted into the game of serious literary criticism. Although from its birth the novel provoked loud and sustained responses, it took nearly two decades for critics to begin seriously peeling the layers Steinbeck insisted were here. Before *The Grapes of Wrath* appeared in print, Steinbeck predicted that the novel would be attacked "because it is revolutionary." He was correct. Initial responses, a kind of popular criticism, were almost exclusively political, a fact inevitable given the volatile political climate of the American West in 1939. As the novel's sales reached 10,000 a week, and over 400,000 the first year, it was denounced by the Associated Farmers of Kern County, California as "obscene sensationalism." It was banned by the Kansas City Board of Education, and copies of the novel were ordered removed from public libraries in East St. Louis and were burned. An editorial writer for the Oklahoma City *Times*, on 4 May 1939, declared the book to be "a morbid, filthily-worded novel!" before admitting that he had not actually read *The Grapes of Wrath* but was reporting on hearsay.[14] Another writer for the same newspaper complained about the "bedraggled, bestial characters" in the novel, while across the Dust Bowl region countless editorials and letters to the editor both attacked and defended Steinbeck's treatment of the Joads. So aroused were emotions in Oklahoma that thirty-six unemployed men and women picketed the state capitol demanding that the governor act to rectify the conditions depicted in Steinbeck's novel. In the most highly profiled criticism of the novel, on 24 January 1940, Oklahoma Conressman Lyle Boren denounced *The Grapes of Wrath* before Congress as a "dirty, lying, filthy manuscript" and "a lie, a black, infernal creation of a distorted mind." "Take the vulgarity out of this book," the congressman stated, "and it would be blank from cover to cover."[15] As late as 1959, a critic was still complaining that *The Grapes of Wrath* was a work that "preaches class warfare and hate."

Reviewers to date have responded to Steinbeck's biggest novel with mixed criticism. To Joseph Henry Jackson, a writer for the *San Francisco Chronicle* and a longtime admirer of Steinbeck's fiction, the novel was "a magnificent book" and completely accurate.[16] Prominent reviewers such as Clifton Fadiman, Malcolm Cowley, Dorothy Parker, and Upton Sinclair reacted very favorably to the novel. A reviewer for the *Los Angeles Examiner,* however, found the novel "pornographic" and the work of "a propaganda-fevered brain," while a *Newsweek* reviewer attacked the novel for its supposed encouragement of agricultural violence.

With a few exceptions, early critics writing about *The Grapes of Wrath* in books or literary journals tended to take an approach oddly similar to that of the letters to Oklahoma newspapers, focusing not on thematic or technical concerns but on the characterizations of the Joads and the other migrants in the novel. Malcolm Cowley, declaring fervently that "A whole literature is summarized in this book and much of it is carried to a new level of excellence," went on to state that "in the Joad family, everyone from Grampa . . . down to the two brats, Ruthie and Winfield, is a distinct and living person."[17] Cowley's contemporary, Edmund Wilson, disagreed, writing that "it is as if human sentiments and speeches had been assigned to a flock of lemmings on their way to throw themselves into the sea."[18] Joseph Warren Beach declared in 1941 that "*The Grapes of Wrath* is probably the finest example produced in the United States of what in the thirties was called the proletarian novel."[19] Social problems in the novel, Beach suggested, are "effectively dramatized in individual situations and characters. . . ."[20] Harry Thornton Moore, author of the first book-length critical study of Steinbeck, *The Novels of John Steinbeck* (1939), disagreed, finding the characters contrived, merely devices through which Steinbeck could voice his own thoughts.[21] Still other early critics referred to the Joads as "puppets," or "marionettes," always, in the words of Alfred Kazin, "on the verge of becoming human." Maxwell Geismar, faintly approving of Steinbeck as one of America's writers of social consciousness, faults Steinbeck's Joads on still other grounds as being "as idealized in their own way as those smooth personages who dwell in the pages of *The Saturday Evening Post.*"[22]

The consensus throughout the first couple of decades of criticism of *The Grapes of Wrath* was that Steinbeck was to be classified as a proletarian, that is, as a writer concerned with the social plight of the worker, and that, in a era still strongly influenced by the naturalism of the late nineteenth and early twentieth centuries, Steinbeck was interested in man as biological phenomenon. If Steinbeck's Joads resembled lemmings in Edmund Wilson's eyes, that was understandable given that the naturalist's interest is in man as a product of Darwinian evolution and as a pawn of biological and psychological forces neither recognized nor comprehended. That Steinbeck was a fairly knowledgeable amateur marine biologist who had published *The Log from the Sea of Cortez* (early and late versions), which explained biological views of man, did nothing to hamper such naturalistic readings.

Whereas Beach had chosen to contrast Steinbeck's idealism with James T. Farrell's naturalism as two poles of "the life of the imagination," Woodburn O. Ross, drawing upon the 1941 *Sea of Cortez, In Dubious Battle,* and *Of Mice and Men,* as well as *The Grapes of Wrath,* declared in a 1949 essay, entitled "John Steinbeck: Naturalism's Priest," that Steinbeck's "new religion" of naturalism was "extremely primitive," and virtually reduced man to animism. Unlike the British romantic Wordsworth, Ross states, "Steinbeck does not see through nature to a God beyond; he hears no intimations of immortality. . . ."[23] As early as 1941, however, in "The Philosophical Joads," Frederic I. Carpenter had pointed out Steinbeck's affinity in this novel with "the mystical transcendentalism of Emerson . . . and the earthy democracy of Whitman, and the pragmatic instrumentalism of William James and John Dewey." The "group idea" espoused in the novel, argued Carpenter, "is that of American Transcendentalism. . . ."[24] In contrast to Ross, Carpenter places Steinbeck, particularly because of the gospel of the preacher Casy, directly in the line of American romanticism. In 1947 Chester E. Eisinger located *The Grapes of Wrath* in still another vein of American thought, Jeffersonian agrarianism, and suggested that if this is Steinbeck's answer in the novel, it is an impractical one.

Following the initial flurry of reviews and sparring between disparagers and defenders of the novel, critical interest in *The Grapes of Wrath* waned. Peter Lisca has pointed out that no more than half a dozen critical essays on *The Grapes of Wrath* appeared in literary journals in the first fifteen years after the publication of the novel. Interest was revived in the early fifties when Bernard Bowron, trying to explain the phenomenon of the novel's lasting popularity, found *The Grapes of Wrath* to be simply another "Wagons West" romance of no great signifiance.[25] Warren French, one of the most discerning of Steinbeck's critics through the years, responded in 1955 with a penetrating critical analysis of the novel, pointing beyond the genre Bowron cited toward the operation of older archetypes from such ancient sources as Exodus and *The Odyssey* in *The Grapes of Wrath*. In 1961 French published his *John Steinbeck*, a volume in Twayne's United States Authors Series, which followed Peter Lisca's 1958 volume *The Wide World of John Steinbeck* as only the second serious book-length critical study of the author since Moore's 1939 work.

Surprisingly, considering the heavy influence of the King James Version of the Bible upon Steinbeck's writing, the Christian elements in the novel received little attention until 1956 when Martin Shockley published a seminal essay entitled "Christian Symbolism in *The Grapes of Wrath*." Shockley argued for a reading of Casy as "a contemporary adaptation of the Christ image" and a reading of the novel "in which the meaning of the book is revealed through a sequence of Christian symbols." Tom Joad, Shockley argued, was Casy's disciple, while Rose of Sharon's act of breast-feeding the starving man in the barn at the novel's end represented the "resurrective aspect of

Christ."[26] Shockley's loose-jointed biblical reading of the novel was quickly criticized in an essay by Eric W. Carlson, who found the novel's symbolism to be primarily "non-Christian" and humanistic.[27] A teapot tempest of argument concerning the possible Christian symbolism and import of the novel followed, with various critics contending that the novel was anything from rigidly Christian in its symbolism to antireligious. One critic, Walter F. Taylor, argued in 1959 that "under cover of a pious social objective a number of other and quite different meanings are slipped past the reader's guard: those of hostility, bitterness, and contempt toward the middle classes, of antagonism toward religion in its organized forms, of the enjoyment of a Tobacco-Road sort of slovenliness, of an easygoing promiscuity and animalism in sex. . . ."[28] With the publication of another book-length study of Steinbeck's work, Joseph Fontenrose's 1963 *John Steinbeck: An Introduction and Interpretation,* the issue of Christian symbolism began to ebb. Fontenrose, classical scholar and symbol/analogue hunter par excellence, documented the religious symbolism in the novel thoroughly if not always convincingly. Furthermore, Fontenrose strongly influenced future Steinbeck criticism by pointing toward the influence in Steinbeck's fiction of the ancient vegetation cults underlying both the Arthurian romances so important to Steinbeck's fiction and the sacrifice and resurrection of Jesus. Readings by both Lisca and French complemented Fontenrose's findings by insisting that the Joads must expand their consciousness in what French terms an "education of the heart" and Lisca a "movement from escape to commitment." J. P. Hunter, in "Steinbeck's Wine of Affirmation in *The Grapes of Wrath,*" added new insights including the suggestion that "As the Joads hover in the one dry place in their world—a barn—the Bible's three major symbols of a purified order are suggested: the Old Testament deluge, the New Testament stable, and the continuing ritual of communion."[29]

The subject of Christian symbolism in the novel was finally set aside, at least temporarily, by Agnes Donohue in " 'The Endless Journey to No End' " with the declaration that "Enough has been made of the biblical analogues in *The Grapes of Wrath*. . . ." Donohue goes on to conclude that the Joads' exodus "out of the wilderness to the land of promise is a journey of initiation into dark knowledge, from life to death."[30]

Neither Steinbeck nor his Dust Bowl novel consented to remain buried as critical subjects, however, because critical analysts in the sixties and seventies began to look more closely at the structural and thematic elements within the novel. In "Machines and Animals: Pervasive Motifs in *The Grapes of Wrath*," Robert J. Griffin and William A. Freedman examined machine and animal in the novel. Paul McCarthy, in a 1967 essay entitled "House and Shelter as Symbol in *The Grapes of Wrath*," and Betty Perez, in "House and Home: Thematic Symbols in *The Grapes of Wrath*" (1972), examine the concept of home and shelter from differing perspectives.[31] In "John Steinbeck: Architect of the Unconscious," an impressive 1972 dissertation, Clifford Lewis explored Steinbeck's fiction from a Jungian perspective. In 1974, Howard Levant published another book-length volume, *The Novels of John Steinbeck: A Critical Study*, a work in which he attempted to look more closely than had previously been done at structural and thematic elements in Steinbeck's fiction and found much lacking in the author's artistry. The lasting popular and critical interest in Steinbeck's fiction was reconfirmed again in 1975 and 1978 as both Warren French and Peter Lisca, respectively, published revised versions of their earlier long studies of Steinbeck's work. 1978 also saw the reprinting of F. W. Watt's 1962 study entitled *Steinbeck*.

Warren French, in a 1976 essay entitled "John Steinbeck and Modernism," took yet another look at the reasons behind Steinbeck's lack of critical popularity, and concluded that when Steinbeck destroyed the early draft entitled "L'Affaire Lettuceberg" he transcended "the ironic detachment of Modernism with a new affirmative conception of individual regeneration."[32] The old question of Steinbeck's historical and cultural accuracy even worked its way back to the surface again, very belatedly, in 1977 in Floyd C. Watkins's *In Time and Place: Some Origins of American Fiction*, in which the critic devotes a chapter to *The Grapes of Wrath* and criticizes Steinbeck for errors in the novel.

Other critics, in essays published in the 1980s, have continued to both delve into old questions and peel back the layers toward new understanding in this novel, examining the subject of matriarchy in the character of Ma Joad or comparing Ma to Hemingway's Pilar; looking at the journey motif (a questing after Eldorado) or arguing for a kind of "Psycho-Physical Questing" as the quintessential journey in the novel; making a case for Jim Casy as a believer in "an earthly millenium [sic] through redemptive labor organizing," and arguing as late as 1986 that Casy is "a sentimentalized abstraction" in a novel that pathetically straddles a fence between collective action and individualism.[33] Finally, in my own 1985 book-length study, *John Steinbeck's Revision of America,* I make a case for *The Grapes of Wrath* as an indictment of the so-called American myth and suggest that Steinbeck, contrary to what had often been claimed, was careful not to sentimentalize his migrant protagonists.

In his 1959 essay, "John Steinbeck: The Fitful Daemon," R. W. B. Lewis made the grand pronouncement that Steinbeck's "career to date has the shape of a suggestive, a representative, and a completely honorable failure," and that the author of *The Grapes of Wrath* "has been accorded the respectful burial which is our contemporary American way of honouring living writers whom we have pretty well decided not to read any longer."[34] *The Grapes of Wrath,* Lewis stated, "does not manage to transcend its political theme. . . ." As essays and books on Steinbeck and *The Grapes of Wrath* continue to flow from word processors and presses, Lewis's epitaph appears premature at best. An astonishing number of readers throughout the world have apparently decided to continue reading this novel as well as other Steinbeck works, and a significant number of critics have begun to move beyond studying content toward a close scrutiny of form and technique in Steinbeck's fiction. *The Grapes of Wrath* would seem, thirty years after Lewis's declaration, to represent a completely honorable success as the layers of the novel continue to offer themselves up to careful study.

A Reading

Jane Darwell, Henry Fonda, and Russell Simpson as Ma, Tom, and Pa Joad in John Ford's film *The Grapes of Wrath*. Courtesy of the Steinbeck Research Center, San Jose State University Library, San Jose, California.

4

The Beginning: The Camera's Eye

The Grapes of Wrath is one of America's great novels and the zenith of John Steinbeck's career; it is a mature, extraordinarily ambitious and balanced statement of the major themes that dominated his life's work. Free of the heavy-handed symbolism and allegorism that could, at times, damage such lesser Steinbeck novels as the early *To a God Unknown* and the late *Burning Bright, The Grapes of Wrath* combines the precise craftsmanship of such shorter works as *In Dubious Battle* and *Of Mice and Men* with the scope and daring of an ambitious and sprawling novel such as *East of Eden.* The result is a tightly unified work of epic dimension whose focus moves smoothly from American people—the Joads and other migrants—to America itself and back again, and brings home to American readers both the intimate reality of the Joad's suffering and the immense panorama of a people's—the Dust Bowl migrants'—suffering. Malcolm Cowley accurately summed up Steinbeck's achievement in this novel when he declared, "A whole literature is summarized in this book and much of it is carried to a new level of excellence."[35]

In responding to editors' criticism of the book's conclusion even before the novel was published, Steinbeck explained: "Throughout

I've tried to make the reader participate in the actuality, what he takes from it will be scaled entirely on his own depth or hollowness. There are five layers in this book, a reader will find as many as he can and he won't find more than he has in himself."[36] While this is a claim many authors would like to make and while authors' declarations are often best taken with large grains of salt, *The Grapes of Wrath* is, like another great American novel, *Adventures of Huckleberry Finn*, a work we can indeed keep peeling for ever more rewarding layers. Much excellent critical analysis has been brought to bear already by such careful readers as Warren French, Peter Lisca, Joseph Fontenrose, Frederic Carpenter, Chester Eisenger, and others. Much exploration, however, remains.

Surprisingly, little critical attention has been directed toward that most logical of starting places: the beginning of the novel. We will start there, with one of the most impressive stylistic accomplishments in American literature.

Paragraph one of *The Grapes of Wrath* opens with an impressionistic swath of color reminiscent of Stephen Crane's *The Red Badge of Courage* as Steinbeck intones, "To the red country and part of the gray country of Oklahoma, the last rains came gently, and they did not cut the scarred earth." He continues:

> The plows crossed and recrossed the rivulet marks. The last rains lifted the corn quickly and scattered weed colonies and grass along the sides of the roads so that the gray country and the dark red country began to disappear under a green cover. In the last part of May the sky grew pale and the clouds that had hung in high puffs for so long in the spring were dissipated. The sun flared down on the growing corn day after day until a line of brown spread along the edge of each green bayonet. The clouds appeared, and went away, and in a while they did not try any more. The weeds grew darker green to protect themselves, and they did not spread any more. The surface of the earth crusted, a thin hard crust, and as the sky became pale, so the earth became pale, pink in the red country and white in the gray country.(1)

The Beginning: The Camera's Eye

A reader familiar with Steinbeck's fiction will note immediately a recurrent technique. Almost invariably Steinbeck begins his novels with a carefully realized setting before introducing his characters into the setting that will in a large part define them. Environment in Steinbeck's fictional worlds imprints itself upon the human inhabitant, and man in turn impresses his character upon that environment. A close look at this paragraph, however, suggests that much more is being accomplished than a simple delineation of place or setting.

The opening line of the novel is broadly panoramic as it evokes "the red country and part of the gray country of Oklahoma. . . ." Following this panoramic, generalized opening, the paragraph begins to focus, to zoom in: "The plows crossed and recrossed the rivulet marks." And finally, from the vague, impressionistic opening image our vision has closed the distance to focus very closely upon not just "the growing corn" but the "line of brown" that spreads "along the edge of each green bayonet." At once the novel's narrative eye begins to pan back to register broader details of clouds and generalized "weeds" until the paragraph ends where it began, with a panoramic image of the earth, which "became pale, pink in the red country and white in the gray country." In the novel's second paragraph, the camera's eye again zooms in for a close-up: "In the water-cut gullies the earth dusted down in dry little streams." And again this paragraph expands to end with a panorama: "The air was thin and the sky more pale, and every day the earth paled."

In these first paragraphs, Steinbeck is showing us the dust-blown landscape inhabited by the Joads and all of the other sharecroppers who will soon become the migrants in this novel. By requiring that our first encounter in the novel be not with his protagonists or with any characters at all, but with nature, or environment, he is conveying a message: the primary forces to be contended with in this novel are enormous, irresistible, as great as the earth itself, which, in fact, is what in sum they are. Inexorability and inevitability brood in the constant winds and dry dust. When man appears in this environment he has already been reduced, made to seem powerless before the epic forces that blow across the land.

Just as importantly, and more subtly, in these opening paragraphs Steinbeck is introducing the pattern upon which his entire novel will be structured: a pattern of expansion and contraction, of a generalized panoramic view of the plight of the migrants in the interchapters, followed, in the narrative chapters, by a close-up of the plight of the representative individuals, the Joads. As early as the novel's opening paragraph the reader is subliminally programmed for this movement in the novel and introduced to the idea that beyond the Joads is the larger phenomenon of the migrants and the Dust Bowl as a whole; beyond the seeming tragedy of the drought and the cropped-out land is the panoramic earth itself. The shifting focus is designed to remind us that the individual tragedies are played out against a backdrop of enduring life. In teleological terms, as defined by Steinbeck and Edward F. Ricketts in *The Log from the Sea of Cortez,* the drought, the Dust Bowl, and the tragedy of the migrants seem immeasurable disasters for which blame must be assigned; in nonteleological terms, however, we are reminded by the panoramic sweep of the author's brush that we are seeing only part of the picture, partial indices of what the *Log* defined as "all reality, known and unknowable."[37]

Paradoxically, such a nonteleological perspective serves to make the Dust Bowl a tragedy only insofar as it is judged according to transient, human values. From a distance, the drought-wasted land is lovely, a sweeping panorama of pastels; up close, the picture becomes one of horror, but only in human terms. For the sharecroppers this is a tragedy; the larger picture suggests that the tragedy is limited, transient, that the earth abides beyond man's errors and short-sightedness. To believe, as the croppers and land owners in this novel do, that one can "kill the land" is to see only part of the picture; they commit the error Joseph Wayne commits in Steinbeck's early novel *To a God Unknown*—that of believing that the land can die. The biblical prose style of these opening paragraphs, recalling the incantatory force of Genesis, also underscores the power of primal creation that precedes man and exists beyond man's ability to affect or effect. Like the people who, drawing their strength from the earth, "go on," as Ma Joad will say later in the novel, the earth cannot be destroyed, and Steinbeck's style and tone in these first paragraphs is designed to reinforce that message.

If Steinbeck's message here is that the land cannot die, he nonetheless begins as early as the first paragraph of the novel to subtly imply a degree of human responsibility for the Dust Bowl disaster. In the novel's second sentence, he tells us that "The plows crossed and recrossed the rivulet marks," superimposing an ultimately self-destructive human pattern—the erosion-inducing furrows—upon the natural watershed pattern. The rivulet marks are a sign of the earth's flow, cycle, continuum; their crossing and erasure is a sign of a failure of human understanding. The wheels that "milled the ground," and the hooves that "beat the ground" until "the dirt crust broke and the dust formed" further underscore man's responsibility for the disaster that is depicted in the first paragraphs and developed throughout the novel. By the novel's end, the rain will come again in a great, destructive, cleansing flood, erasing in its turn the pattern of human failure impressed upon the Edenic valleys of California.

Steinbeck also foreshadows the fate of the migrants in these opening paragraphs. The "weed colonies," which are "scattered . . . along the sides of the roads," suggest the colonies of migrants that will soon be scattered the length of Route 66; and the minuscule ant lion trap, a funnel of finely blown sand from which the ant simply cannot escape, is a naturalistic image that serves to define the situation of the sharecroppers. (In chapter 19 the mass of migrants will be compared explicitly to "ants scurrying" across the West.) The sharecroppers have no future in the cropped-out region of blowing dust and sand; they have sealed their fates should they stubbornly struggle to remain. Muley Graves, whose name hints strongly at his character and fate, chooses to remain in the trap, a "graveyard ghos' " without a future.

Through this burnt country cut the tracks of walking men and men's machines, which raise dust clouds as signs of their passage. When Tom Joad appears, he will be the representative walking man, the individual who must learn to accept responsibility for what man has done to himself and to the earth. Along with Tom, the Joads and all of the migrants will be sent on the road on a quest to rethink their relationship with both humanity and the land itself. It is a process that Steinbeck critic Warren French has aptly termed the "education of the heart."

Thus, in a few paragraphs, Steinbeck has set the stage for his characters, introduced ingeniously the structural pattern of his novel, defined the dimensions of the forces with which his characters must contend, and suggested man's responsibility for the place he inhabits. Immediately we will see the novel's structure laid out in the movement between narrative chapter—the story of the Joads—and interchapter—the story of the people as a whole. We will see the inexorability of the sharecroppers' eviction from this land, the irresistibility of the forces arrayed against them and the unmistakable culpability of the croppers. All of this is foreshadowed in one of the most brilliant beginnings in American literature.

5

Participation and Education:
The Narrative Structure

In attempting to write the story of a human tragedy on a national scale, Steinbeck was faced with a dilemma. Documentaries, a genre with which Steinbeck was thoroughly familiar, tended to give the big picture, the suffering of multitudes, with the effect that the viewer or reader was both educated and at the same time distanced from the intimate suffering and pain of those caught up in the disaster under scrutiny. "It means very little to know that a million Chinese are starving unless you know one Chinese who is starving," Steinbeck wrote in 1941 in the preface to his script for the documentary, *The Forgotten Village*. In the same preface Steinbeck added:

> A great many documentary films have used the generalized method, that is, the showing of a condition or an event as it affects a group of people. The audience can then have a personalized reaction from imagining one member of that group. I have felt that this was the more difficult observation from the audience's viewpoint. . . . In *The Forgotten Village* we reversed the usual process. Our story centered on one family in one small village. We wished our audience to know this family very well, and incidentally to like it, as we did. Then, from association with this little personalized group, the larger

conclusion concerning the racial group could be drawn with something like participation.[38]

"Something like participation" is what Steinbeck desired for *The
Grapes of Wrath*. The reader must not only be shown the enormity of
the widespread suffering, he must also identify with the migrants, and
feel on a personal level their loss, their hope, their frustration and
futility, their enduring strength. It is this participation in the lives of
the Joads that will capture the reader and carry him through the experience of a long novel, and it is only through this participation that
the full emotional impact Steinbeck desired can be achieved. In order
to involve the reader on this kind of immediate, intimate level Steinbeck invented a single family upon which the story could focus. Steinbeck intended for the reader to take the Joads to heart, and to identify
with this one struggling family, in all their warm-blooded, quixotic,
flawed humanity. The anguish of the Dust Bowl migration and the
torments in California will then be not just the migrants' but the readers' as well.

The real subject of the novel, however, was not the suffering of a
single family. For the novel to be successful, the reader must be aware
that the Joads are only selected specimens, that there are thousands of
others just like the Joads, and that what Steinbeck is writing about is
a tragedy on an enormous, epic scale.

In order to communicate both the intimate, personalized suffering
and the sense of large-scale, generalized suffering Steinbeck—influenced by John Dos Passos's narrative experimentation in the novel
U.S.A.—evolved the structural strategy of two kinds of alternating
chapters for *The Grapes of Wrath*. The narrative chapters thus follow
the migration of the Joads, telling their personal story of pain and
despair and hope, while the interchapters shift the narrative consciousness from the intimate portrait of the Joads to the epic dimensions of
the Dust Bowl tragedy.

Of the thirty chapters in *The Grapes of Wrath,* sixteen, less than
twenty percent of the novel's word-count, are what Steinbeck called
intercalary chapters, or interchapters. Beginning with the novel's first
chapter, these narrative interludes allow the narrative eye to pan back,

away from the intimate picture for a broad view of generalized experience. The Joads are allowed to appear in none of the interchapters, which Steinbeck referred to as "repositories of all the external information" in the novel. Not only do the interchapters give us the broad picture of the migrants' suffering, they also provide necessary background information such as the history of agriculture in California.

Steinbeck adopts several techniques for ensuring that his novel will not simply fall into two parts—narrative chapter and interchapter. Chapter 1, for example, introduces the setting and the generalized picture of the Dust Bowl, with faceless sharecroppers looking up at the clouds or watching the dust blow, lying in bed and listening to the silence when the wind dies. The chapter ends with a very faint, barely felt note of promise as Steinbeck writes, "As the day went forward the sun became less red. It flared down on the dust-blanketed land" (4). The generic sharecroppers squat in doorways "thinking—figuring." Chapter 2 picks up the dying color of the sun-burdened land in the first line: "A huge red transport truck stood in front of the little roadside restaurant" (4). From the waning fire-tone of the dust-laden sky to the vital red of the powerful truck is a significant transition. The dying red of the sky and the aggressive red of the truck couple the twin threats of nature and machine, threats that will be underscored as the dust continues to blow and the tractors begin to cut through dooryards and doorways doing the work of a score of men and horses and making the tenant farmers useless. Very faintly, through touches of color, Steinbeck has created here a transition between the end of the first impersonal "interchapter" chapter and the beginning of the first narrative chapter in which we will meet Tom Joad, the novel's protagonist.

In the first chapter we are told of a "walking man" who lifted a thin layer of dust as he moved. In chapter 2 that faceless walking man, one of thousands that exist in a land of new homeless, becomes personalized in "a man walking along the edge of the highway . . ." (5). The individualized walking man of chapter 2 is Tom Joad, who will quickly find a way to make the powerful machine, the red transport truck, work for him as he inveigles the truck driver into giving him a ride to his family's farm. An important connection between the face-less sharecroppers in the first chapter and the Joads, whom we will soon meet, is further established when the driver asks of Tom's father, "A forty-acre cropper and he ain't been dusted out and he ain't been tractored out?" (8).

Chapter 3, the second interchapter, contains Steinbeck's cele-brated description of the "land turtle," a creature that crawls carefully and inexorably across a dry land surprisingly replete with life:

> The concrete highway was edged with a mat of tangled, broken, dry grass, and the grass heads were heavy with oat beards to catch in a dog's coat, and foxtails to tangle in a horse's fetlock, and clover burrs to fasten in sheep's wool; sleeping life waiting to be spread and dispersed, every seed armed with an appliance of dispersal, twisting darts and parachutes for the wind, little spears and balls of tiny thorns, and all waiting for animals and for the wind, for a man's trouser cuff or the hem of a woman's skirt, all passive but armed with appliances of activity, still, but each possessed of the anlage of movement. (14)

The turtle, "turning aside for nothing," overcomes the obstacle of a roadside embankment, is avoided by one driver and deliberately run over by another. The truck that hits it, however, merely flips the turtle further in the direction it was already moving. Once it has righted itself again, the turtle continues indomitably on its way, accidentally burying as it moves across the earth a "wild oat head" that had be-come caught up in its shell.

The turtle is an unmistakable symbol for the migrants. As critics have pointed out, the turtle, like the Joads and other migrants, carries its home as it travels. Like the migrants, it must hazard life on the road, and, like the migrants, it faces a hostile world of machinery. Finally, like the migrants, the turtle goes on despite obstacles and haz-ards, carrying new life in the form of the oat seed across the highway, and planting that new life on the other side. Much later in the novel, after they have traveled the length of Route 66 and arrived in the land of promise, Ma Joad will declare, "The fambly hadda get acrost" (252), a phrase designed to call to mind not only the desert crossing of the Israelites fleeing from bondage in Egypt, but also the crossing of the turtle. Also, later in the novel the narrative voice of the inter-chapters will warn those who "hate change and fear revolution" that in the mass movement toward California "is the anlage of the thing you fear" (165). Again, in the word "anlage," the symbolic turtle and the migrants are linked.

With the naturalistic symbol of the turtle, Steinbeck has made it clear that the migrants will succeed in carrying new life into the new land. Like the land turtle, although they will suffer, they cannot fail. The drying, dust-bearing wind that blows seeds across the land will also uproot and spread the migrants along the length of Route 66 to California, strewing new life across the West. Conveyed exclusively through natural imagery and prefiguring the ultimate success of the migration, chapter 3 becomes the story of the Joads and the migrants in microcosm.

In Chapter 4, the novel's second narrative chapter, Tom Joad discovers a land turtle and rolls it up in his coat as a present for the younger Joads. Immediately, the necessary connection between the interchapter detailing the turtle's struggle and the narrative chapter detailing Tom Joad's movement homeward is established. Steinbeck underscores this connection with still more subtle devices. In the first paragraph of the chapter Tom's walk is described: "Joad took a few steps, and the flourlike dust spurted up in front of his new yellow shoes, and the yellowness was disappearing under gray dust" (17). Three paragraphs later, when Tom Joad spots the turtle, we are told that "The back was brown-gray, like the dust, but the underside of the shell was creamy yellow. . . ." Through color again—of shoes and shell—Steinbeck associates Tom with the indefatigable turtle. It is not Tom alone, however, who is associated visually with the turtle. When the ex-preacher, Jim Casy, appears in this chapter we are given one of the quick descriptive sketches at which Steinbeck excels:

> Joad had moved into the imperfect shade of the molting leaves before the man heard him coming, stopped his song, and turned his head. It was a long head, bony; tight of skin, and set on a neck as stringy and muscular as a celery stalk. His eyeballs were heavy and

protruding; the lids stretched to cover them, and the lids were raw and red. His cheeks were brown and shiny and hairless and his mouth full—humorous or sensual. The nose, beaked and hard, stretched the skin so tightly that the bridge showed white. . . . The strained bundle of neck muscles stood out. (19)

It is difficult not to note Casy's resemblance to the turtle described in Chapter 3, a resemblance Casy himself heightens when he tells Tom, "Nobody can't keep a turtle. . . . They work at it and work at it, and at last one day they get out and away they go—off somewheres. It's like me" (21). When, in chapter 6, the turtle gains its freedom, it "headed southwest as it had been from the first," its journey inter-rupted but unbroken as it moves in the same direction the Joads will take when they depart for the promised land of California.

Chapter 4 ends with Tom and Casy looking down at the deserted Joad homestead as Tom cries, "Looka that house. Somepin's hap-pened" (31). Chapter 5, the third interchapter, comes in response to this declaration by Tom, showing us through dramatization what the "something" is that has happened to the Joads and to countless other croppers in the region. In this chapter we hear the voices of faceless "owner men" and "tenant men" in lines of dialogue made impersonal by the absence of quotation marks. Here we see acted out the gener-alized drama through which the croppers are driven from the land. We see the representative cropper briefly confront "Joe Davis's boy" as the latter prepares to drive a tractor through the farmhouse doorway, and we experience the generalized futility as the farmer steps aside. When we come to chapter 6, we find that the Joad house has been crumpled at one corner and, because the previous chapter has prepared us to do so, we easily envision the scene that must have taken place in the Joad farmyard just as it did in countless others. Muley Graves, who has elected to remain with the useless land, informs Tom that Tom's grandpa has confronted the tractor driver and shot the headlights out of the tractor before stepping aside. And here, in Muley's story, the name of the driver is changed from Joe Davis's boy to Willy Feeley, suggesting that identical dramas are being enacted throughout the stricken country, and that others have turned on their own people for the sake of individual survival.

Again and again, Steinbeck shows us the big, documentary picture in the interchapter—the selling of property and the purchase of a rattletrap car or truck, the migration westward—and then personalizes the same picture by focusing on the Joads. In chapter 7 we are taken to a used car lot on the edge of one of countless small towns in the Dust Bowl region and we experience through a rapid cacophony of language and dizzying movement of imagery the confusion of the sharecropper who has come to this alien environment to pay too much of his meager savings for an unreliable vehicle. When, in chapter 8, we see the Joad's cut-down sedan in Uncle John's dooryard, we know immediately that the generalized experience of chapter 7—the confusion, fear, and bewilderment of the car lots—has been their experience as they bargained for the make-shift truck. Just as importantly, however, through the preceding interchapter we know their experience has been that of innumerable others.

Steinbeck unifies the narrative chapters and interchapters by linking actions and experiences—what the universal sharecropper or migrant experiences, the Joads experience; what the Joads experience, others experience. He links the chapters through voice as well, at times using the idiomatic expressions that characterize the Joads not only in the narrative chapters but also within the interchapters from which the Joads are excluded. And he exploits unifying imagery to achieve a coherence, particularly through images of animals and machines, as the examples of the turtle and the tractors and automobiles demonstrate.

Thematically, as Peter Lisca has pointed out, the novel is structured in three parts: the time in the cropped-out, wind-blasted Dust Bowl; the time on the road; and the time in California where the novel ends. Lisca sees this tripartite division as corresponding to the three stages of the biblical Exodus: the Israelites' time in bondage, where God has sent plagues to force the Egyptians to free them (chapters 1–11 in the novel); the forty years of wandering in the desert wilderness (chapters 12-18); and the arrival in Canaan, the Promised Land (chapters 19–30). "The plagues in Egypt, which released the Israel-ites," Lisca adds, "have their parallel in the drought and erosion in Oklahoma; the Egyptian oppressors, in the bank officials; the hostile Canaanites, in the equally hostile Californians."[39]

Another structural principle operating within the novel, one that corresponds roughly to the principle of expansion-contraction be-tween the two kinds of chapters, is the pattern of loss and gain that occurs as the Joads and the other migrants are transformed from a disorganized movement of isolated families into a mass movement of what Steinbeck terms "Manself." Within this pattern of loss and gain, the Joads face constant reduction as a family, losing first Grampa and then Granma to death, losing Noah to the enticing waters of the Col-orado River, Connie to the attractions of going it alone, Al to mar-riage, and Tom to his commitment to the larger good. Finally, in the novel's closing tableau, the Joads have been reduced by more than half. In counterpoint to this pattern, as the Joads are reduced as a family they become increasingly a part of the larger whole as they begin to identify with the mass of migrants moving westward; they incorporate first Casy and then the Wilsons and finally, near the nov-el's end, the Wainwrights, and at the same time they are absorbed into the mass migration.

An additional function of the interchapters is that of offsetting the intimacy of the narrative chapters, of creating necessary distance between the reader and Steinbeck's representative family. Despite his desire that we feel the emotional impact of the Joads' story, Steinbeck uses the interchapters skillfully throughout most of the novel as a means of preventing the reader from identifying too closely with the Joads and thereby losing his sense of the larger dimensions of the trag-edy. Again and again, just as we begin to be drawn fully into the pain of the Joads' experience, Steinbeck pulls us away from the intimate picture and into the broad scope of one of the interchapters, reminding us that these are merely representative people, that the scale of suffer-ing is so great as to dwarf the anguish of one small group such as Ma Joad's family. Chapter 18 ends, for example, with the Joads about to descend into the promised land of California's Central Valley, weighted with the emotionally charged burden of the dead grandmother. In this most poignant of scenes, the heartbreaking courage of Ma, who has lain beside Granma all night to ensure that the family gets "acrost," is deeply moving, and as the Joads prepare to drive down into the highly stylized Eden of the Valley the reader must respond emotionally to the courage and suffering of the family. Immediately, however, in the opening lines of chapter 19, Steinbeck shifts the reader's attention away from the Joads and onto a broad, impersonal sweep of California's agricultural history culminating in a view of the Hoovervilles and a generic portrait of the migrants.

The Joads' suffering is put into perspective. The opening line of chapter 19 tells us that "Once California belonged to Mexico and its land to Mexicans; and a horde of tattered feverish Americans poured in" (254). Immediately we become aware that the Joads and the other migrants are part of a pattern so large they cannot comprehend it, a pattern of land usurpation driven by land hunger: the Mexicans took it from the Indians, and the Americans from the Mexicans. Steinbeck writes, "The Mexicans were weak and fled. They could not resist, because they wanted nothing in the world as frantically as the Americans wanted land" (254). Eventually, the Americans, too, soften: "And the hunger was gone from them, the feral hunger, the gnawing, tearing hunger for land. . . ." Now they, like the Mexicans, are ripe for despoilation of their holdings by a new migration of more feverish claimants. It is the pattern of American settlement, that which led the farmers to drive Indians from the plains and which has led them here to contest the richness of California with the banks and corporations.

With these lines the implicit promise is made that the migrants, who want land as feverishly as the original settlers, will be victorious. And Steinbeck goes beyond the pattern of American history to place the phenomenon of the migration in the context of world history. "What if they won't scare?" the representative "owner" voice asks in rising fear. "What if some time an army of them marches on the land as the Lombards did in Italy, as the Germans did on Gaul and the Turks did on Byzantium? They were land-hungry, ill-armed hordes too, and the legions could not stop them" (260–61). And to make, once again, the connection between the migrants and the American pattern, Steinbeck has his representative migrant voice repeat the refrain from chapter 5: "Grampa took his lan' from the Injuns" (261). The historical pattern transcends the Dust Bowl and America; it is the pattern of human history, and Steinbeck implies that the owners should be aware of the pattern:

> And the great owners, who must lose their land in an upheaval, the great owners with access to history, with eyes to read history and to know the great fact: when property accumulates in too few hands it is taken away. And that companion fact: when a majority of the people are hungry and cold they will take by force what they need. And the little screaming fact that sounds through all history: repression works only to strengthen and knit the repressed. The great owners ignored the three cries of history. (262)

The owners fail to realize, in Steinbeck's words, that "Paine, Marx, Jefferson, Lenin were results, not causes." And within this grand scheme of history, the Joads become infinitesimally small.

On a more intimate level, we realize once again that the Joads' tragedy is every migrant's, that there must be a thousand Granmas and as many Ma Joads, and that the family is about to descend into a sea of families in precisely the same circumstances, families facing their predicament with roughly the same proportion of courage and cowardice. In place of the familiar voices of Tom and Ma Joad the reader now hears the voice of history, and the perspective is readjusted once again. It is more difficult to become sentimental about the fate of the individual when one is simultaneously aware of the fate of the species.

The plunge from Tehachapi Pass with the Joads is a plunge away from melodrama and into history with all its matter-of-factness. In the overall pattern of American expansion and world history, the Dust Bowl migration is simply another phenomenon that "is," that must be seen in a larger cultural and historical context. Here, the documentary sweep of the novel reaches epic proportions immediately upon the heels of the most touching personal moment in the novel.

Participation and Education: The Narrative Structure

If Steinbeck works hard throughout most of the novel to ensure necesary distance from the Joads, and a corresponding objective detachment in the reader, near the novel's conclusion he begins to move in the other direction. It is finally necessary that the two kinds of chapters consistently create a single coherent effect, culminating in chapters 29 and 30, which provide first a broad panorama of the incessant rains and rising flood waters, followed by a focus upon the Joads in the midst of the flooded land. By concluding with the Joads, Steinbeck both ensures that his novel will end on an intimate, personal note that deeply involves the reader and also provides a final note of balance between interchapter and narrative chapter. The novel begins with a broadly panoramic picture from which the Joads are excluded and it ends with such a chapter (29), followed by the final narrative chapter that features the Joads. As he reads the last lines of the novel, the reader is allowed no opportunity to remove himself from the personal tragedy of the Joads, the intimately human suffering.

Steinbeck ensures that the reader will be plunged deeply into the Joads' story by steadily increasing, in the final third of the book, the proportion of the novel devoted to the Joads. Whereas the first narrative chapter, chapter 2, is approximately eleven pages long—taking up slightly more space in the text than does the first interchapter (chapter 1)—by chapter 20 the narrative chapter has grown to fifty-seven pages in comparison to the preceding interchapter, chapter 19 with its eleven pages. Succeeding narrative chapters, telling the increasingly tense story of the Joads, will reach lengths of fifty-five (chapter 22) and seventy-five pages (chapter 26). In counterpoint, the final five interchapters will average approximately four-and-one-half pages.

As the interchapters begin to form a more abbreviated and urgent counterpoint to the lengthening narrative chapters, Steinbeck manipulates the novel's structure to prevent the story from becoming too documentary and impersonal. Here, as the novel moves toward the family's heroic struggle with the flood and Rose of Sharon's ultimate act of charity, more intense involvement with and longer exposure to the Joads is required of the reader, in order to bring about the necessary identification and thus the emotional charge of the final scene. Steinbeck swings the novel's momentum squarely into the Joads' camp with chapter 26, which carries the Joads from the brief idyll of the Weedpatch episode to the ominous atmosphere of the Hooper Ranch, and finally to Casy's death, Tom's murder of Casy's killer, and the family's relocation in the boxcar camp where Tom hides in the culvert.

Almost twice as long as all but two of the other narrative chapters, chapter 26 carries a heavy burden. It must advance the action through major events—Casy's death, Tom's revenge and separation from the family—and it must serve as a convincing transition into the novel's denouement. As the crisis chapter, it bridges several hundred pages of gradually rising action and the few remaining pages of resolution. With impressive efficiency Steinbeck moves Tom closer to Casy and prepares for Tom's role as the preacher's disciple. He also foreshadows Rose of Sharon's conversion from irritable self-centered child to Ma-like mother of the world when he causes Ma, at a point of despair for Rose of Sharon, to pierce her daughter's ears and pass on to the girl the mother's symbols of womanhood—the gold earrings. Following this rite of passage, Rose of Sharon makes her first unselfish gesture of the novel when she tells the injured Tom, "You jus' sleep off. I'll watch the door. They won't nobody get in" (436).

6

The Biblical Joads

The two works most influential in Steinbeck's writing, from beginning to end, were Malory's *Morte d'Arthur* (from which came Steinbeck's fascination with King Arthur and the grail quest) and the King James Version of the Bible. While the grail quest of Arthurian Romance is central to other Steinbeck works it plays no significant role in *The Grapes of Wrath*; however, the novel depends heavily upon and is powerfully influenced by the Bible—from the title to the final scene.

As a number of critics, such as Peter Lisca, Martin Shockley, and Joseph Fontenrose, have made clear, Christian allusions and symbols are numerous in *The Grapes of Wrath*. The novel's title, for example, is taken from "The Battle Hymn of the Republic" ("He is trampling out the vintage where the grapes of wrath are stored") and emphasized in the jeremiad in chapter 25 of the novel, "In the souls of the people the grapes of wrath are filling and growing heavy, growing heavy for the vintage" (385). At the same time, this is an allusion to Revelation, in which the wine of God's wrath figures prominently in prophecies of the Apocalypse: "And the angel thrust his sickle into the earth, and gathered the vine of the earth, and cast it into the great winepress of the wrath of God" (Rev. 14:19), and ". . . Babylon is fallen, is fallen that great city, because she made all nations drink of the wine of the wrath of her fornication," and "If any man worship the beast and his image . . . The same shall drink of the wine of the wrath of God. . . ." (Rev. 14:8,9). Attributing the title to his first wife, Carol, Steinbeck wrote his agent Elizabeth Otis to say, "I think it is Carol's best title so far. I like it because it is a march and this book is a kind of march— because it is in our own revolutionary tradition and because in reference to this book it has a large meaning."[40] In order to ensure that his readers make this important connection, Steinbeck insisted that the entire score of the "Battle Hymn" be printed inside the cover of the novel.

The "large meaning" Steinbeck felt in the title very likely stemmed from the crucial convergence of symbols found in the three words and their source. Within the title come together suggestions of both the nation's revolutionary beginnings and its religious underpinnings, just as in the lines from Revelation underlying the song merge implications both of the Eucharist, with its sense of a forgiving God, and of apocalypse and a punishing, Calvinistic deity. All of these elements become important in understanding the novel as a work not about the Joads or the migrants alone, but about the nation as a whole, a nation founded, even as a loose collection of colonies, upon ideas of Eden and apocalypse, religious tolerance and a vengeful God.

Of greatest significance within the range of biblical symbols, of course, is that of Christ, represented in the novel not only by Jim Casy but also by Tom Joad and even Rose of Sharon. Christ, it must be remembered, came as a herald of a new consciousness, as a leader for the oppressed masses, and as a sacrificial figure whose death would offer man a new beginning and a second chance. Jim Casy, with his eye-catching initials, is such a Christ figure in this novel. Like Christ, Casy has gone into the desert to wrestle with his faith, or as Casy puts it, "Here's me, been a-goin' into the wilderness like Jesus to try find out somepin" (421). And like Christ, Casy has discovered within himself a commitment to mankind. Twice Casy is described as glowing with light, the second time, just before he is killed, he is identified as "That shiny bastard." And it is Casy who says, an instant before he is murdered, "You don' know what you're a-doin' " (426) in an echoing of Christ.

Casy's new religion marries Christian commitment and a sensual celebration of the life-force, as the song he is singing when we meet him suggests. To the tune of "Yes, Sir, That's My Baby," Casy is singing, "Yes, sir, that's my Saviour, / Je—sus is my Saviour, / Je—sus is my Saviour now" (18). Like the palimpsest in Steinbeck's later novel *The Wayward Bus*—the bumper sticker on Juan Chicoy's bus that reads "Sweetheart" but overlays an older sticker reading "*el Gran Poder de Jesus*"—this song celebrates both the spiritual and the sensual, and defines Casy's orientation toward life.

Other biblical parallels of varying significance noted by critics include the fact that twelve Joads set out with Casy toward the uncertain future, just as twelve disciples followed Christ. The name Joad recalls the tribe of Judah; Connie Rivers, who deserts, is not really a Joad and through his betrayal suggests Judas; the grapes of California's Central Valley call to mind the cluster of grapes attesting to the promise of Canaan in the Bible, as well as the grapes of God's wrath; the dust that settles over everything suggests one of the plagues God sent upon Egypt; the Colorado River, which the Joads bathe in before crossing the ominous desert, figures as a handy Red Sea with which the Israelites put bondage behind them. And there are more similarities: the first names of the Joads—two named Thomas, one John—and Casy's name—James—are the names of Christ's disciples; the three dollars a day (thirty dimes) paid to the tractor driver to betray his people equal the thirty pieces of silver paid to Judas; the rooster that crows the night of Casy's death recalls the rooster that crowed before the Crucifixion. In addition, two Joads have still more suggestively biblical names, Noah and Rose of Sharon, allusions which will be discussed later in this study in our consideration of the novel's conclusion.[41]

If it seems obvious that Jim Casy is the Christ figure of this novel, however, we are forced nonetheless to take Tom Joad into account. It is Casy who has baptized Tom Joad, just as John the Baptist baptized Jesus, and it is Tom, we are told, who was called "Jesus Meek" while in prison. If Tom is thus to be identified with Christ, Casy may be a John the Baptist figure crying out in the wilderness and prefiguring Christ's role as savior, as is suggested when Ma Joad watches the preacher as though he were "a voice out of the ground" (89). It is Tom who in the process of being symbolically reborn into the man of the people, repeatedly crawls into womb-like caves throughout the novel. He sleeps in a cave in Chapter 6; he hides in the cave of the mattress after he has killed Casy's murderer; and he finally crawls out of the cave of vines when he has become dedicated to all men. It is Tom who, like Christ, teaches in parables when he tells the one-eyed junkyard caretaker stories of a one-legged whore and a hump-back. When the man responds with, "Well, Jesus, ya see somebody edge away from ya, an' it gets into ya," the connection with Christ seems rather obvious. While "Jesus" may be a common epithet, it is difficult to ignore the suggestion that the man, listening to Tom's teaching, is addressing him as Jesus. It is Tom of whom Ma Joad says, "I knowed from the time you was a little fella. . . . They's some folks that's just theirself an' nothin' more. There's Al—he's jus' a young fella after a girl. You wasn't never like that, Tom. . . . Ever'thing you do is more'n you. . . . You're spoke for" (389).

The answer may be that both Casy and Tom Joad are Christ figures, that Steinbeck often deliberately blurs the parallels in order to isolate not one individual but the Christian impulse toward commitment and self-sacrifice within all men. When Casy and Tom meet in the desert of the cropped-out and dusted-our farmland, their relationship is cemented with a sacrament: "Joad took the bottle from him, and in politeness did not wipe the neck with his sleeve before he drank" (20). From this point until late in the novel Casy will be the teacher, Tom the student. In the end, Tom will go out to spread the gospel of Casy.

To understand the function of the Christian parallels in the novel, and to avoid the unnecessary wrangling that has long taken place regarding Steinbeck's use of Christian symbols within the novel, we must look to *The Log from the Sea of Cortez*, where Steinbeck and his longtime friend, marine biologist Edward F. Ricketts, offer their definition of religion: "And it is a strange thing that most of the feelings we call religious, most of the mystical outcrying which is one of the most prized and used and desired reactions of our species, is really the understanding and the attempt to say that man is related to the whole thing, known and unknowable."[42]

It is this "mystical outcrying" that forms the center of Jim Casy's philosophy throughout the novel, articulated in Casy's declaration that "There was the hills, an' there was me, an' we wasn't separate no more. We was one thing. An' that one thing was holy" (88). This "one thing" is further defined in the *Log* as "the one inseparable unit man plus his environment." Reminiscent, as critics have long ago pointed out, of Emerson's concept of the transcendental Oversoul, this intuitive sense of oneness and commitment is what Steinbeck is writing about in *The Grapes of Wrath*.

Throughout Steinbeck's fiction, Christ figures proliferate: Jim Nolan in *In Dubious Battle,* Juan Chicoy in *The Wayward Bus* (whose initials are the same as Casy's), Hazel in *Cannery Row,* Jesus Maria in *Tortilla Flat,* Ethan Allen Hawley (also a Judas figure) in *The Winter of Our Discontent,* Thomas Wayne in *To A God Unknown*. The aspect of Christ's nature that Steinbeck is inevitably concerned with in these parallels, however, is the impulse toward commitment to the larger whole, a commitment demonstrated through self-sacrifice. And the larger whole includes "all reality," the earth as well as mankind, the ecological whole.

Steinbeck, as his representation of the "Jehovites" and "Jesus-lovers" in *The Grapes of Wrath* demonstrates, has little use in his fiction for formal religion and even less for rigid fundamentalism. What Casy has left behind in renouncing his former calling is illustrated in the preacher in chapter 23 who labors beside an irrigation ditch: "And the preacher paced like a tiger, whipping the people with his voice, and they groveled and whined on the ground. He calculated them, gauged them, played on them, and when they were all squirming on the ground he stooped down and of his great strength he picked each one up in his arms and shouted, Take 'em, Christ! and threw each one in the water. . . . and he prayed that all men and women might grovel and whine on the ground (365). Casy has given up this fundamentalist preaching, a variation on the Calvinism upon which the New England colonies were founded, declaring that "There ain't no sin and there ain't no virtue. There's just stuff people do. It's all part of the same thing. And some of the things folks do is nice, and some ain't nice, but that's as far as any man got a right to say" (24). Casy goes on: "I figgered about the Holy Sperit and the Jesus road. . . . I figgered, 'maybe it's all men an' all women we love; maybe that's the Holy Sperit—the human sperit—the whole shebang. Maybe all men got one big soul ever'body's apart of" (24).

While there is indeed a strong echo here of Emerson, more important as far as the development of Steinbeck's thought and the thematic development of this novel are concerned is the fact that Casy's new, not fully articulated philosophy suggests precisely the kind of "mystical outcrying" defined in the *Log from the Sea of Cortez*. Casy, who is in the process of committing his life to that of the people as a whole, is attempting to express an intuitive sense of belonging to "the whole thing, known and unknowable," a profound awareness that transcends the kind of judgmental morality he professed as a "Burning Busher" fundamentalist preacher. In going on the road with the Joads, Casy is traveling the "Jesus road" toward knowledge and self-sacrifice in California.

The Grapes of Wrath is the story of a people growing through ignorance and failure and isolation toward a commitment to something much larger than the isolated self. The ignorance includes a failure of responsibility toward the land—the earth has been misused, cropped out, greedily exploited—and toward one's fellow man. The Joads begin the novel as a nuclear family concerned only with their own welfare. They are paragons of American individualism; they embody the pioneer spirit which has driven out and killed the Indian and claimed the land in the name of despoilment. Until Casy joins them in the family council and then on the trek to California, there is a sense that no one exists for the Joads outside of the immediate family. Casy serves as the wedge that begins to open up the Joads, and particularly Ma Joad, to an awareness of the necessity for commitment to something beyond the family. Ma fights throughout the novel to keep the family intact, even threatening Pa with a jackhandle to keep the family unit together. Even Tom comes but reluctantly to a comprehension of Casy's philosophy. Only in the novel's final pages when he has become an outcast and, like Cain, is marked for his double crime of fratricide and forced to wander the land, does Tom dedicate himself to mankind, and put on Casy's mantle.

The biblical parallels in *The Grapes of Wrath* serve to broaden the scope of the novel. On one level it is the story of a family's struggle for survival in the Promised Land—and it must be remembered that the Promised Land was once thought to be all of America and it only gradually retreated westward toward California. On another level it is the story of a people's struggle, the migrants'. On a third level it is the story of a nation, America. On still another level, through the biblical parallels, both the allusions to Christ and those to the Israelites and Exodus, it becomes the story of mankind's quest for profound comprehension of his commitment to his fellow man and to the earth he inhabits.

7

The American Joads

That Steinbeck should keep the Bible firmly in both the background and the foreground of this great American novel is essential, for he is writing not simply about an isolated historical and sociological event—the Dust Bowl and the "Okie" migration—but about a nation founded solidly upon a biblical consciousness, as the novel's title indicates. From the first writings of the colonial founders, America was the New Canaan or New Jerusalem, and the colonists, such as William Bradford's pilgrims at Plymouth, were the chosen people who consciously compared themselves to the Israelites. Their leaders were repeatedly likened to Moses, for they, too, had fled from persecution and religious bondage in England and Europe for the new promise of a place called America. Thus Bradford, in *Of Plymouth Plantation* (1620–50), felt compelled to compare his pilgrims to "Moyses & the Isralits when they went out of Egipte."[43] Out of this acutely biblical consciousness arose what has come to be called the American myth, a kind of national consciousness with which Steinbeck was fascinated throughout his life.

Within this mode of thought, if America was the New Eden, within the wilderness of that Eden lurked the Serpent. Almost at once, in their battle to wrest a continent away from wilderness and from the inhabitants of that wilderness, the colonists imagined themselves embroiled in a desperate struggle with Satan. They saw themselves as the Army of Christ. The Indian in the forest, in resisting the colonists' invasion, appeared to be in league with Satan himself. In his book *The Wonder-Working Providence of Sion's Savior in New England*, describing without compunction the beheading of Pequot Indians, Captain Edward Johnson, in 1653, exhorted the Puritans to "take up your arms and march manfully on till all opposers of Christ's kingly power be abolished."[44]

In *The Grapes of Wrath* Jim Casy has spent his life prior to our meeting with him as just such a Calvinistic fire-and-brimstone fundamentalist embattled with Satan, as he tells Tom Joad: "Here's me that used to give all my fight against the devil 'cause I figured the devil was the enemy. But they's somepin worse'n the devil got hold a the country" (421). It is in the wilderness that Casy has his revelation about man and God, and quickly he moves from Calvinism to a kind of transcendentalism, from that pattern of thought which places the earth under man's dominion and looks at wilderness as the unreclaimed haunt of Satan to that philosophy which makes man inseparable from the natural world and finds in wilderness a direct relationship with truth.

From his past battle with the devil to his declaration that "There was the hills, an' there was me, an' we wasn't separate no more" (88), Casy has taken an enormous stride away from what Steinbeck defines in this novel as the short-sighted and destructive historical pattern of American thought and settlement. Within the Christ-like Casy, commitment to man and to nature becomes a single driving force toward a unity with what Steinbeck and Ricketts in *The Log from the Sea of Cortez* defined mystically as "the whole thing, known and unknowable."

The settlement of America may be seen as a process of ever westward expansion in search of that Eden which seemed to recede always before the eyes of the first colonists. The process became one of despoiling the Garden in the search for the Garden until, finally, Americans stood at the edge of the Pacific, having slaughtered and driven from their lands the original inhabitants, having deforested enormous portions of the continent, and having fought and gouged with all other claimants to the continent in order to reach the western shore. Surely, if there were ever to be a Garden it must be at the western edge. And the beauty and fecundity of California seemed to fulfill that promise. Still, Americans were left with a feeling of loss, emptiness, summed up in Walt Whitman's great poem, "Facing West from California's Shores," in which he concludes with a parenthetic question that resounds throughout American history and American literature: "But where is what I started for so long ago? / And why is it yet unfound?"

Whitman's question is central to *The Grapes of Wrath*. Grampa exclaims, "Gonna get me a whole big bunch of grapes off a bush, or whatever, an' I'm gonna squash 'em on my face an' let 'em run offen my chin" (90). And the faceless, representative owner voices of chapter 5 advise the evicted tenants, "Why don't you go on west to California? There's work there, and it never gets cold. Why, you can reach out anywhere and pick an orange" (35). Both Grampa's dream of grapes and the owners' vague visions of plenty underscore the crucial association between California and the biblical Canaan. And when the Joads arrive at Tehachapi Pass and look down on the fertile San Joaquin Valley, often referred to as the Great Central Valley, California indeed seems to be the New Canaan, the Promised Land sought after for nearly four centuries:

> They drove through Tehachapi in the morning glow, and the sun came up behind them, and then—suddenly they saw the great valley below them. Al jammed on the brake and stopped in the middle of the road, and, "Jesus Christ! Look!" he said. The vineyards, the orchards, the great flat valley, green and beautiful, the trees set in rows, and the farm houses. And Pa said, "God Almighty!" The distant cities, the little towns in the orchard land, and the morning sun, golden on the valley. . . .
>
> Ruthie and Winfield scrambled down from the car, and then they stood, silent and awestruck, embarrassed before the great valley. The distance was thinned with haze, and the land grew softer and

softer in the distance. A windmill flashed in the sun, and its turning blades were like a little heliograph, far away. Ruthie and Winfield looked at it, and Ruthie said, "It's California." (250)

It is Winfield who puts the valley into perspective and locates it firmly within the American dream of Eden rediscovered: " 'There's fruit,' he said aloud" (251).

When a rattlesnake crawls across the road and Tom drives over it and crushes it as the family starts down into the valley, the way has been cleared for entry into the Garden; the serpent—the symbolic evil of this Promised Land—has at long last been removed. To emphasize the quintessentially American idea of a new beginning, a kind of return to the Garden, Steinbeck has Tom laugh and say, "Jesus, are we gonna start clean! We sure ain't bringin' nothin' with us" (254). With these words, Tom defines the most dangerous flaw within the dream of America as the new beginning: the Joads, like the Dutch sailors who look longingly at the continent at the end of F. Scott Fitzgerald's *The Great Gatsby*, and like all of us, are indeed bringing their pasts with them. This Garden is inhabited by flawed men, men who, like Tom with his scar at the novel's end, are marked. The Eden- and Canaan-like valley that spreads so wonderfully beneath the Joads will prove to be filled with hatred, violence, greed, and corruption—the fruits of man's wisdom and knowledge lying rotting in the fields and orchards. It is a heavily ironic entrance into the Promised Land.

Steinbeck's use of and fascination with what has been termed the American Myth—the myth of this continent as the new Eden and the American as the new Adam—appear again and again throughout his fiction. *Cup of Gold* (1929), Steinbeck's first novel, offers a fictionalized account of the pirate Henry Morgan's conquest of Panama. The primary symbol of this new world in the novel is the chalice or golden cup that suggests the Holy Grail. Purity, promise, and innocence all come together in the symbol of the Grail but, as Steinbeck's conqueror discovers, the New World—America—loses its innocence in the process of being discovered. In *The Pastures of Heaven*, (1932) Steinbeck's early episodic novel, the author makes a small California valley a microcosm for America and the people of that valley, with their fatal insistence upon a kind of illusory innocence, microcosmic Americans. Characters in that novel (Steinbeck's second published though third written) look upon the valley called Pastures of Heaven and they dream of starting over in all innocence, of leaving their flawed selves and the fallen world behind. Steinbeck's message in the novel, of course, is that such illusions of innocence are impossible to realize and dangerous to harbor. Fallen man brings his own flaws into Eden.

Throughout his career, Steinbeck was obsessed with America as a subject. The myths deeply ingrained in our national consciousness and the patterns of thought that have carried us from wilderness to world power appear again and again in Steinbeck's writing, not only in such obvious studies of the nation as *America and Americans* or *Travels with Charley,* but also throughout the novels.

In *The Short Reign of Pippin IV* (1957), Steinbeck, like Henry James before him, but on a lighter note, takes a young "ideal" American to France in order to contrast the public and private moralities of the two nations. Four years later, in his final novel, *The Winter of Our Discontent,* Steinbeck turns his scrutiny squarely upon his own nation in a dark study of the American conscience. Here, Steinbeck evokes American history in the name of his protagonist, Ethan Allen Hawley, who lives in a home with "Adam" decorations. Again Steinbeck creates in Ethan a character who refuses, as long as possible, to recognize humanity's flaws. And in the most allegorical of his major novels, *East of Eden* (1952), Steinbeck creates an explicit American Adam in the character of Adam Trask, who, in a self-destructive search for his own unfallen Eden, flees from his Calvinistic, Jehovah-like father on the eastern seaboard and settles in the Salinas Valley in California.

Steinbeck recognized deep within the American and the universally human psyche a need to believe in the possibility of beginning anew, of returning symbolically from the exile of maturation and experience to a lost Eden and lost innocence. The original English colonists saw America very consciously as this new Eden, and Americans have ever since translated that dream of recovering Eden into the American dream, the dream of shedding the past and starting over.

For Walt Whitman this meant an outright denial of original sin, a chance to proclaim himself Adam—the representative American—newly born into innocence. For Benjamin Franklin it meant a chance to create oneself in the pattern of one's imagination, free of any burden of guilt. It is no coincidence that, as a boy, Fitzgerald's Gatsby wrote notes to himself reminiscent of Benjamin Franklin's *Autobiography*. It is this refusal to see the evil we do and the belief in an Eden just west of the next mountain range that Steinbeck saw as the most dangerous flaw in the dream. In *East of Eden*, Adam Trask refuses to see the evil within his wife or within others. He is doomed by that self-willed innocence.

In *The Grapes of Wrath*, Steinbeck evokes this pattern of American thought and American expansion, a pattern that begins with thoughts of a new Eden and moves inexorably westward. This is the illusory hope voiced by a representative migrant in one of the novel's interchapters: "Maybe we can start again, in the new rich land—in California, where the fruit grows. We'll start over" (95). The impossibility of such a dream is made clear in the answering voice: "But you can't start. Only a baby can start. . . . The bitterness we sold to the junk man—he got it all right, but we have it still. And when the owner men told us to go, that's us; and when the tractor hit the house, that's us until we're dead. To California or any place—every one a drum major leading a parade of hurts marching with our bitterness" (95).

Steinbeck takes pains to place the Joads and the Dust Bowl migrants as a whole securely within this pattern of American history and simultaneously to avoid the sin with which he has often been charged: sentimentalizing his characters. Certainly Steinbeck makes it clear that the sharecroppers are victimized by an inhuman economic monster—personified by the enormous, impersonal tractors raping the land—that tears at the roots of the agrarian life Thomas Jefferson so highly prized for Americans. When Steinbeck causes his representative migrant voice to plead with the owners for a chance to remain on the land, however, he qualifies the celebrated Jeffersonian agrarianism and love-for-the-land in this novel by tainting the sharecroppers' wish: "Get enough wars and cotton'll hit the ceiling" (32), the cropper ar-

gues. While the reader is likely to sympathize with the powerless tenant farmer, the tenants' willingness to accept war and death as the
price for a chance to remain on their farms and thus further "cotton
out" the land is difficult to admire on any level.

Steinbeck goes a step further, to make it clear that the migrants
are firmly fixed in a larger, even more damning American pattern.
Though the tenants have tried to persuade the owners to let them hang
on, hoping for a war to drive up cotton prices, the tenant voice also
warns the owners: "But you'll kill the land with cotton." And the owners reply: "We know. We've got to take cotton quick before the land
dies. Then we'll sell the land. Lots of families in the East would like
to own a piece of land" (33). It is the westering pattern of American
history laid bare: people arrive on the Atlantic seaboard seeking Eden
only to discover a rocky and dangerous paradise with natives who
aggressively resent the "discovery" of their land; Eden must lie ever to
the west, over the next hill, across the next plain; then only the Pacific
Ocean is there and, along with Jody's grandfather in Steinbeck's *The
Red Pony,* we end up shaking our fists at the Pacific because it stopped
us, and broke the pattern of displacement. As long as we believe there
is a Garden to the west we feel justified in using up and abandoning
the place we inhabit today. Tomorrow we will pick up and go, always
in the direction of the setting sun, always with the belief that we can
put the past behind us, that the ends will be justified by the means.
We believe that such acts as passing out smallpox-infested blankets to
Indian tribes and the massacre at Wounded Knee and, finally, the theft
of the continent from the Indians can be put behind us in the quest for
new land and new self.

That the croppers are part of this pattern becomes even more
evident when the representative tenant voice informs us that their fa-
thers had to "kill the Indians and drive them away." And when the
tenant voice adds, "Grampa killed Indians, Pa killed snakes for the
land" (34), Steinbeck is attempting to ensure that we hear a powerful
echo of the Puritan forebears who wrested the wilderness from the
serpent Satan and his Indian servants, killing and displacing the original inhabitants of the New Canaan.

It is difficult to feel excessive sorrow for these ignorant men who are quite willing to barter death to maintain their place in the destructive pattern of American expansion—a pattern that has ravaged a continent. That Steinbeck thought long about the American phenomenon of destroying the Garden in the search for the Garden is suggested in his declaration (recorded more than a decade later in *Journal of a Novel,* the journal he kept while writing his great investigation of the American myth, *East of Eden*) that "people dominate the land, gradually. They strip it and rob it. Then they are forced to try to replace what they have taken out."[45]

Although Steinbeck makes it clear that man draws sustenance from close contact with the earth, through touching it and feeling a part of it, and in spite of Tom Joad's final wish that the people will one day "all farm our own lan' " (463), Steinbeck is not making a case for Jeffersonian agrarianism in this novel. Jeffersonian agrarianism, as defined succinctly by Chester E. Eisinger in his influential essay "Jeffersonian Agrarianism in *The Grapes of Wrath,*" was "essentially democratic: it insisted on the widespread ownership of property, on political and economic independence, on individualism; it created a society in which every individual had status; it made the dignity of man something more than a political slogan."[46] Drawing parallels between Thomas Jefferson's insistence upon the small farmer as the foundation of an ideal society and the philosophy developed in *The Grapes of Wrath,* Eisinger suggests that "Steinbeck was concerned with democracy, and looked upon agrarianism as a way of life that would enable us to realize the full potentialities of the creed."[47]

The "essentially inhuman and unproductive nature of the machine age," according to this reading of the novel, is destroying "a way of life that was based on the retention of the land."[48] Such a reading, while persuasive, leads even Eisinger to question the value of agrarianism itself: "It remains to inquire if agrarianism, its form and substance, is the part of the Jeffersonian tradition that we should preserve."[49] The Jeffersonian ideal is bankrupt, the critic declares, and thus Steinbeck's conclusions in the novel are of dubious value.

If we look more closely at attitudes toward America and, in particular, the small farmer in *The Grapes of Wrath,* it should become clear that Steinbeck, too, saw fully illuminated the "bankruptcy of Jefferson's ideal." By carefully and precisely placing the tenants within the historical pattern that has led to the destruction of the land, Steinbeck is making it obvious that agrarianism alone is insufficient. In fact, the ideal of the independent small farmer, the Jeffersonian image of the heroic individualist wresting an isolated living from the soil, is very firmly scuttled in *The Grapes of Wrath*. Muley Graves points to an aspect of this failure when he tells Tom and Casy, "I know this land ain't much good. Never was much good 'cept for grazin'. Never should a broke her up. An' now she's cottoned damn near to death" (50).

The small farmers of this novel proudly proclaim their grandparents' theft of the land from the Indians, freely acknowledging that murder was their grandparents' tool. They argue that they should be allowed to stay on and raise more cotton because war will boost the price of cotton. Then they tell the owners that they will kill the land with cotton. These small farmers are far from anyone's ideal. They are clearly a part of a system that has failed and in the process has violated the continent. Steinbeck sends them on the road so they may discover a new relationship with their fellow man and with the land itself. The Jeffersonian ideal is one of individuals working the land on isolated farms; Steinbeck's ideal is one of all men working together, committed to man and land, to "the whole thing." It is, in fact, precisely the dangerous idea of man as isolated and independent that Steinbeck is attempting to expose. He is no Jeffersonian.

Once the Joads and their fellow migrants have reached California, they can go no farther. The Joads are the representative migrants, and the migrants are the representative Americans. The migrants' westward journey is America's, a movement that encapsulates the directionality of the American experience. The horrors confronting the migrants to the California Eden have been brought on by all of us, Steinbeck implies; no one is innocent. When, near the novel's conclusion, Uncle John places Rose of Sharon's stillborn baby in an apple box and releases it upon the flood waters with the words, "Go down an' tell 'em" (493), Steinbeck is emphasizing the new consciousness. This Moses—in the Edenically suggestive apple box—is stillborn because the people have no further need for a Moses. There is no Promised Land and nowhere else to go, no place for a Moses to lead his chosen people. The American myth of the Eden ever to the west is shattered, the dangers of the myth exposed. The new leader will be an everyman, a Tom Joad, who crawls into a cave of vines—the womb of the earth—to experience his rebirth, who emerges committed not to leading the people somewhere but to making this place, this America, the garden it might be. This is the Tom who, early in the novel, says to Casy, "What the hell you want to lead 'em someplace for? Jus' lead 'em" (21).

At the novel's end, Tom has become such a leader, one who will not lead the people "someplace" but will lead them toward a new understanding of the place they inhabit here and now. For the same reason, Steinbeck has left Noah behind at the Colorado River, the boundary of this garden, because, in spite of the impending flood, there is no place for a Noah in the new country. Two symbols of mankind's new beginnings from the Bible are rejected in the exclusion of Noah and the stillborn Moses. Through these two rather heavy-handed allusions, Steinbeck is declaring that there is no second chance, no starting over.

The Grapes of Wrath is Steinbeck's jeremiad, his attempt to expose not only the actual, historical suffering of a particular segment of our society, but also the pattern of thought, the mind-set, that has led to far more than this one isolated tragedy. In this novel, with the Bible very much in mind, Steinbeck sets out to expose the fatal dangers of the American myth of a new Eden, and to illuminate a path toward a new consciousness of commitment instead of displacement. And in making his argument, Steinbeck is careful not to sentimentalize his fictional creations, careful to emphasize the shared guilt and responsibility—a new sensibility, not sentimentality, is Steinbeck's answer.

In spite of howls of outrage from the states at the opposite ends of the novel's journey—both Oklahoma and California—however, and in spite of his care to avoid sentimentalizing his characters, America took the Joads to heart, forming out of *The Grapes of Wrath* a new American archetype of oppression and endurance. And in spite of his care to make the Joads and the migrants as a whole far less than perfect, and to place his protagonists squarely within the destructive pattern of American expansion, as soon as the novel was published critics who read less carefully than they should have began to accuse Steinbeck of sentimentality in his portrayal of the downtrodden migrants. Edmund Wilson was one of the first influential critics to take such a position, declaring that in this novel Steinbeck learned much from films, "and not only from the documentary pictures of Pare Lorentz, but also from the sentimental symbolism of Hollywood." [50] Bernard De Voto had anticipated Wilson when he complained that the novel's ending was "symbolism gone sentimental."[51] Still a third major American critic, R. W. B. Lewis, found Steinbeck's fiction "mawkish" and "constitutionally unequipped to deal with the more sombre reality a man must come up against. . . ."[52]

There is much in *The Grapes of Wrath* to ward off such accusations if a reader goes beyond mere surface story. In addition to showing the reader the tenant farmers' willingness to continue to use up the land with cotton and their eagerness for war, Steinbeck consistently shows us the flaws in his characters. As Steinbeck scholar Warren French pointed out long ago, Steinbeck takes care to undercut the nobility and "goodness" of the migrants. Although Casy, in sacrificing himself for the people, and Tom, in dedicating his life to the same cause, move close to heroism, no one in the novel is seen through a sentimental lens.

One of the most obvious examples of Steinbeck's care to avoid sentimentality can be found in the novel's final chapter. Just before the Joads reach the barn and discover the starving man and young boy, Ruthie discovers a "scraggly geranium gone wild." Plucking the flower, she sticks one of the petals onto her forehead, "a little bright-red heart." With this symbol of delicate beauty and love surviving amidst the devastation of ravaged and ravaging nature, Steinbeck could have left his reader with a soft and sentimental portrait-in-miniature of hope. Instead, he deftly undercuts the sentimentalism of the moment through the verisimiltude of his characters. "Come on, Ruthie!" the girl's younger brother, Winfield, begins at once to whine, "Lemme have one." Ruthie, in keeping with the character the reader has come to expect, "banged him in the face with her open hand" (498). A moment later she "wet a petal with her tongue and jabbed it cruelly on his nose. 'You little son-of-a-bitch,' she said softly" (499). In the children's attraction toward the bright-red petals Steinbeck illuminates an image of the enduring life-force and the wellspring of hope in the novel. In Ruthie's convincing cruelty the author refuses to allow his characters to succumb to the potential sentimentalism inherent in the image. The romantic symbol and its ironic deflation prepare for the novel's emotional and critically controversial finale.

8

"Grampa Killed Indians, Pa Killed Snakes": The American Indian and *The Grapes of Wrath*

As is suggested above, the presence of the American Indian in *The Grapes of Wrath* is a significant and little noted one. Given the two-fold concern that runs through this novel, both for the American myth and for the kind of intuitive sense of oneness with nature expressed through Jim Casy, it is inevitable that the Indian will haunt the shadows of this American epic.

An abstract, often romantic concept of "Indianness" permeates Steinbeck's writing, from *Cup of Gold*, his first novel, through nearly all of his major works. Perhaps the best example of what Steinbeck defined as Indian can be found in *The Pearl*, the author's 1947 novella portraying a conflict between an Indian community and the more sophisticated and shrewd world of Spanish Mexico. As Indians, Kino and Juana in *The Pearl* represent for Steinbeck a profound and intuitive connection with the natural world. From that novel's opening line, "Kino awakened in the near dark," until their tragic encounters with death in a dark range of mountains, Kino and Juana operate in a kind of prelapsarian state of unenlightened innocence, functioning primarily on the level of the unconscious as the primal pair in the timeless, unfallen world of their village. We are told in the opening paragraphs, for example, that the couple awakens to "a morning like other mornings yet perfect among mornings."

In this version of what we might call mythic naturalism, faced with the inexorable forces of civilization, the Indian protagonists are nearly destroyed by their simplicity and naïveté. For Steinbeck these Mexican Indians are purely symbols, walking shadows illustrating the kind of intuitive, nonrational state he and Ricketts celebrate in the Indians they described in *The Log from the Sea of Cortez*:

> They seem to live on remembered things, to be so related to the seashore and the rocky hills and the loneliness that they are these things. To ask about the country is like asking about themselves. "How many toes have you?" "What toes? Let's see—of course, ten. I have known them all my life, I never thought to count them. Of course it will rain tonight, I don't know why. Something in me tells me I will rain tonight. Of course, I am the whole thing, now that I think about it. I ought to know when I will rain."[53]

The picture painted here in the *Log* is a narrowly romantic one, a portrait of a simple people in a simple, uncomplicated world. Similarly, Juanito in Steinbeck's *To a God Unknown,* Pepé in "Flight," Danny in *Tortilla Flat,* Juan Chicoy in *The Wayward Bus,* and old Gitano in "The Great Mountains" are, among other Steinbeck characters, of mestizo, or mixed-blood heritage, and the traces of Indian blood Steinbeck injects into these characters signify only one thing: they have a more profoundly intuitive nature. The Indian, Steinbeck seems to suggest again and again, exists on a less rational, more harmoniously intuitive basis than does his Anglo-European counterpart. When this element is passed on to the mixed-blood, the result is both a deeply mystical response to the natural world and a conflict between rational and non-rational selves. As a result of Steinbeck's attitude there is a kind of dreamy celebration in Steinbeck's stories and novels of a romantic element definable as "Indianness" along with a familiar foreboding of inexorable doom for the Indian. When, for example, Danny, the paisano protagonist of *Tortilla Flat,* wanders down to stare off the pier "into the deep, deep water," he is staring into the dark depths of his unconscious. In the end, the "primitive" Indian self that would lead Danny back toward the forest and the simple life is embattled with the European self that would urge him toward the civilized world. Danny's conscious and unconscious selves are in conflict, and that conflict destroys him.

Most often, Steinbeck chooses to deal with flesh-and-blood "Indianness" in the form of the Mexican or Mexican-American, and in this somewhat remote, exotic form for Steinbeck the Indian need not actually be dealt with as anything more than an impulse, a shadowy presence. On the other hand, when he chose to notice the North American Indian, Steinbeck shifted ground considerably. The Indian blood enriching Mexico and Mexican-Americans serves invariably as a sign of profound, unconscious impulses, a link to the mystical. The Native American, however, tens of thousands of whom lived in Steinbeck's California during his lifetime and live there still, exists in Steinbeck's fiction purely as an index to the American Myth.

As noted above, this version of the Steinbeck Indian is introduced in *The Grapes of Wrath* when the representative sharecropper cries, "Grampa killed Indians, Pa killed snakes for the land." In this novel, the Indian is of significance only as a symbol of the destructive consciousness underlying American settlement and the westering pattern. He has mythic dimension but no further reality. When, late in the novel, the migrants gather in the evenings, Steinbeck writes: "The story tellers, gathering attention into their tales, spoke in great rhythms, spoke in great words because the tales were great, and the listeners became great through them" (445). Here, in this romantic, epic tradition, one storyteller recalls Indian fighting on the frontier:

> They was a brave on a ridge, against the sun. . . . Spread his arms an' stood. Naked as morning, an' against the sun . . . Stood there, arms spread out; like a cross he looked. . . . An' the men—well, they raised their sights an' they felt the wind an' couldn' shoot. Maybe that Injun knowed somepin. . . . An' I laid my sights on his belly, 'cause you can't stop a Injun no other place—an'—then. Well, he jest plunked down an' rolled. An' we went up. An' he wasn' big— he'd looked so grand—up there. All tore to pieces an' little. Ever

see a cock pheasant, stiff and beautiful, ever' feather drawed an' painted, an' even his eyes drawed in pretty? An' bang! You pick him up—bloody an' twisted, an' you spoiled somepin better'n you . . . you spoiled somepin in yaself, an' you can't never fix it up. (360)

Here, naked against the sun, with arms raised in Christ-like cruciform, the Indian as symbol cuts to the heart of the idea America has of itself. In wilderness—James Fenimore Cooper's temple of nature or Henry David Thoreau's Walden—we may come closest to an unmediated spirituality, to that "part and particle of God" within the isolated self. The Indian, elemental, immersed in the fertile heart of the American wilderness garden, stands for that potential which Americans have sought for more than three centuries.

In this portrait the Indian shadows something within the American consciousness, but beyond this he has no existence and, for all the heroic grandeur of the description, he has no more human dimension than does a pheasant. The conflict between the divided self, which destroyed Danny in *Tortilla Flat,* is located implicitly within the American consciousness in *The Grapes of Wrath.* In attempting to destroy the Indian, Steinbeck suggests, Americans damaged, if not destroyed that element within themselves that connected them with the earth, the intuitive self.

At the story's end, the migrants reflect on the storyteller's picture: "Against the sun, with his arms out. An' he looked big—as God." As long as the Indian remains an abstraction—something intuitive Americans kill within themselves—the much uglier reality of the genocidal slaughter and oppression of real human beings can be kept at a distance. And Steinbeck does this in *The Grapes of Wrath.* The migrants—and Steinbeck's readers—can feel the loss of a connection with something "big"—as big as God, or nature—but in the end they mourn for their own loss or diminishment, not for the actual people killed or driven from the land.

The Grapes of Wrath is indeed an unmistakable jeremiad; it is Steinbeck's warning that America got off on the wrong foot and had better learn new ways of inhabiting the continent that is rapidly being destroyed. The Dust Bowl is of immediate concern in the novel, of course, but Steinbeck makes it abundantly clear that the Dust Bowl is merely one result of a destructive pattern of thought that begins with the Puritan need to identify with Old Testament myths. By finding a convenient place for the Indian in this Old Testament pattern, the conquering colonists found it easy to kill Indian and serpent alike, tainting their newfound Eden in the process of reclaiming it. The Indian as pure idea is Steinbeck's reminder of where America began to go wrong. The Indian as a real, twentieth-century person—unlike Steinbeck's migrants—has little relevance.

Given geographical realities, it was inevitable that a large number of Native Americans would come west with the Dust Bowl migration from Oklahoma—from the region once set aside as "Indian Territory"—and Steinbeck acknowledges this fact in *The Grapes of Wrath* in the form of two Cherokees. When the migrants celebrate a moment of security with the pleasures of a square dance, and Steinbeck's chameleon prose rises brilliantly to the occasion, it is a "Cherokee girl" among the conservative migrant women who abandons herself to the music in a pagan frenzy: "Look at her pant, look at her heave," Steinbeck writes, going on to describe the "Texas boy and the Cherokee girl, pantin' like dogs an' a-beatin' the groun'" (364).

And when the guardians of the Weedpatch labor camp need someone with unusually keen senses to watch the gate during a dance, they choose Jule, a half-Cherokee mixed-blood. Never one to mince words, Tom Joad notes "the hawk nose and high brown cheek bones and the slender receding chin" and says, "They say you're half Injun. You look all Injun to me." Jule replies, "Jes' half. Wisht I was a full-blood. I'd have my lan' on the reservation. Them full-bloods got it pretty nice, some of 'em" (375). In spite of his obsessive interest in the mysterious quality of "Indianness" throughout his writing, nowhere in Steinbeck's fiction does the presence of a real Native American, a flesh-and-blood Indian existing in the present-day world with all of its complexities, come so clearly to life as in this scene. Here, for an instant in Steinbeck's work, a present-day American Indian is made to share in the real difficulties of American life. The Indian, for a brief moment, steps out of the world of shadow and into the mundane light of reality. It is somewhat unfortunate, however, that Steinbeck, a writer who took extreme pains to be factual and accurate in his details, did not bother to learn more about his subject in this case. Either Jule is unusually ignorant of both his rights and the current status of Cherokee tribal lands, or, as is more likely, Steinbeck is uninformed. It seems that Steinbeck was not aware of the realities of the 1887 Allotment Act (Dawes Act), which divided tribal land holdings and eventually transferred more than ninety million acres from Indian to white control. Under the terms of this act, a half-blood such as Jule would be entitled to the same acreage as a full-blood. Had Steinbeck done his customary research, he would also have known that the Cherokee reservation had long since ceased to exist.

But what is important here is not Steinbeck's factual errors but that, once again, the Indian enters Steinbeck's fiction as an idea, a cliché: when the square dance begins to approach the level of a primal ritual with intensely sexual overtones, the female of choice is an Indian—throughout American literature, the white man's guide into the primeval forests of the unconscious; when extrasensory perception—a "Hawkeye"—is needed, the choice is also an Indian.

In his other vast book about the American myth, *East of Eden*, Steinbeck would again invoke the Indian as idea and self-reflection. Of the native inhabitants of northern California, Steinbeck writes grimly in *East of Eden*: "First there were Indians, an inferior breed without energy, inventiveness, or culture, a people that lived on grubs and grasshoppers and shellfish, too lazy to hunt or fish. They ate what they could pick up and planted nothing. They pounded bitter acorns for flour. Even their warfare was a weary pantomime."[54] We can give Steinbeck the benefit of the doubt here and assume that the narrative consciousness of *East of Eden*, a consciousness that will develop and change greatly in the course of that novel, is parroting at this moment the kind of insensitive, blind ethnic chauvinism necessary in the original settlers who displaced and killed the Indians. From such a perspective the narrative voice mimics the national consciousness that rationalized its treatment of the Indian, the same national consciousness invoked in *The Grapes of Wrath*.

Of the "Indian fighting" in the late nineteenth century—the process through which sharecroppers of *The Grapes of Wrath* acquired the land they hold so dear—Steinbeck writes in *East of Eden*: ". . . the tribes were forced into revolt, driven and decimated, and the sad, sullen remnants settled on starvation lands. It was not nice work, but given the pattern of the country's development, it had to be done."[55] Here, Steinbeck's aim is to place Adam Trask—*East of Eden*'s protagonist—squarely within this cruel and destructive pattern, and here again the Indian serves as an index to Adam's Americanness. Steinbeck must make his character representative of America itself, the so-called American Adam. To do so he must place Adam securely within the westering pattern he had laid out more than a decade earlier in *The Grapes of Wrath*, a pattern that requires the displacement and decimation of the American Indian.

In *The Grapes of Wrath*, a novel that on one crucial level cries out at injustice, the figure of the Indian is index and symbol but no more. In Steinbeck's great novel, as in most American literature, the Indian remains merely an abstraction, an "Injun Joe" mirror reflecting back at America its own fantasies and its own guilt. The real Indian is finally subsumed, through the vehicle of literature, into the self-consciousness of white America that is portrayed in this novel, becoming that America's shadow and ceasing to exist in his own right. That this transformation should take place within the pages of *The Grapes of Wrath* should be no surprise, for surely this is the most quintessentially American of novels.

9

"Manself" in the Promised Land:
From Biology to Bible

In a letter to a friend just before writing *In Dubious Battle* (1936), Steinbeck said, "You must have heard about the trickiness of the MOB. Mob is simply phalanx, but if you try to judge a mob by the nature of its men units, you will fail just as surely as if you tried to understand a man by studying one of his cells."[56] *In Dubious Battle*, Steinbeck's novel about a violent strike by fruit pickers in a small northern California valley, is Steinbeck's most explicit attempt to explore the nature of what he called "group man," individuals who have joined in a larger movement of men and have thus surrendered their identities and wills to the collective will of the mass. A character in that novel, Doc Burton, says, "A man in a group isn't himself at all, he's a cell in an organism that isn't like him any more than the cells in your body are like you. . . ." [57]

The concept of phalanx, or "group man," fascinated Steinbeck throughout the thirties and grew out of the author's preoccupation with man's biological nature. As early as June 1933 Steinbeck wrote in a letter: "The fascinating thing to me is the way the group has a soul, a drive, an intent, an end, a method, a reaction and a set of tropisms which in no way resemble the same things possessed by the men who make up the group."[58] And almost a decade later, in *The Log from the Sea of Cortez*, Steinbeck and Ricketts would write:

> There are colonies of pelagic tunicates which have taken a shape like the finger of a glove. Each member of the colony is an individual animal, but the colony is another individual animal, not at all like the sum of its individuals. Some of the colonists, girdling the open end, have developed the ability, one against the other, of making a pulsing movement very like muscular action. Others of the colonists collect the food and distribute it, and the outside of the glove is hardened and protected against contact. Here are two animals, and yet the same thing—something the early Church would have been forced to call a mystery. . . . So a man of individualistic reason, if he must ask, "Which is the animal, the colony or the individual?" must abandon his particular kind of reason and say, "Why, it's two animals and they aren't alike any more than the cells in my body are like me. I am much more than the sum of my cells and, for all I know, they are much more than the division of me."[59]

And of a school of fish, the *Log* declares:

> We cannot conceive of this intricacy until we are able to think of the school as an animal itself, reacting with all its cells to stimuli which perhaps might not influence one fish at all. And this larger animal, the school, seems to have a nature and drive and ends of its own. It is more than and different from the sum of its units. If we can think in this way it will not seem so unbelievable that every fish heads in the same direction, that the water interval between fish and fish is identical with all the units, and that it seems to be directed by a school intelligence. If it is a unit animal itself, why should it not so react?[60]

In the opening chapters of *The Grapes of Wrath*, we see the Joads as a small, isolated unit, the family. In the crisis, the family seems to become a single unit resembling the colonial animal or school described in the *Log*: "The people too were changed in the evening, quieted. They seemed to be a part of an organization of the unconscious. They obeyed impulses which registered only faintly in their thinking minds" (108). As a whole, the family comes first, as Ma makes clear when she threatens Pa in order to keep the family together on the road, saying "What we got lef' in the worl'?. . . . All we got is the family unbroke" (185–86).

From the outset of the migration to California, however, the family begins to change as the nuclear family that Ma holds so dear begins to fragment and the Joads begin to become part of a larger "organization of the unconscious." The first step in this gradual change is the family's inclusion of Casy in the council and on the journey. The final steps are Tom's dedication of his life to all men and Rose of Sharon's breast-feeding of the starving stranger. Between these two ends, Steinbeck makes it clear that the Joads have become part of something much larger than themselves.

Ma hints at the metamorphosis in store for the migrants when she says early in the novel, "I got to thinkin' an' dreamin' an' wonderin'. They say there's a hun'erd thousand of us shoved out. If we was all mad the same way, Tommy—they wouldn't hunt nobody down . . ." (83). Casy adds a mystical note to the concept of mass man when he says, his first words echoing Ma's, "I got to thinkin' how we was holy when we was one thing, an' mankin' was holy when it was one thing. An' it on'y got unholy when one mis'able little fella got the bit in his teeth an' run off his own way, kickin' an' draggin' an' fightin'. Fella like that bust the holiness. But when they're all workin' together, not one fella for another fella, but one fella kind of harnessed to the whole shebang—that's right, that's holy" (88). And once the Joads get started on their quest, the family begins almost at once to merge with a larger whole. In chapter 13 the family takes in the Wilsons, an isolated pair of evicted sharecroppers more vulnerable to the life-eroding wear of the road. In chapter 16, Steinbeck writes, "Joads and Wilsons crawled westward as a unit. . . . Joads and Wilsons were in flight across the Panhandle. . . . (222). Omitting the definite articles (*the* Joads) serves to erase distinctions between Joads and Wilsons here. Like collective nouns, "Joads" and "Wilsons" become representative of larger, vaguely defined units, suggestive of the mass movement of migrants pouring over the same route.

In chapter 14 Steinbeck has created a term for this collective whole with a single, driving desire: "Manself." And of the gradually changing nature of the migrant stream he writes, adapting terminology from biology texts:

> One man, one family driven from the land; this rusty car creaking along the highway to the west. I lost my land, a single tractor took my land. I am alone and I am bewildered. And in the night one family camps in a ditch and another family pulls in and the tents come out. The two men squat on their hams and the women and children listen. Here is the node, you who hate change and fear revolution. Keep these two squatting men apart; make them hate, fear, suspect each other. Here is the anlage of the thing you fear. This is the zygote. For here "I lost my land" is changed; a cell is split and from its splitting grows the thing you hate—"We lost *our* land." The danger is here, for two men are not as lonely and perplexed as one. And from this first "we" there grows a still more dangerous thing; "I have a little food" plus "I have none." If from this problem the sum is "We have a little food," the thing is on its way, the movement has direction. . . . This is the beginning—from "I" to "we." (165)

The choice of the word "zygote" and the scientific concept of mitosis applied to the formation of a group consciousness both indicate that Steinbeck is applying the perspective of a scientist to the phenomenon of the Dust Bowl migration. Here, as within the novel as a whole, Steinbeck achieves a unique fusion of the objective tone and stance of the detached, scientific observer with the deeply sympathetic and involved tone of the humanist and social critic. From this combination of profound sympathy for the migrants with an objective, nonsentimental posture comes much of the unique power of *The Grapes of Wrath*; Steinbeck brilliantly balances two seemingly antithetical positions.

As the families move westward, Steinbeck demonstrates their growing ability to merge into larger units with similar needs, pains, and desires. "The families," Steinbeck writes, "which had been units of which the boundaries were a house at night, a farm by day, changed their boundaries" (215). Families join and "a new unit was formed"

(217). And at night, sharing what they have and what they need but lack, "manself" forms a collective whole: "And now the group was welded to one thing, one unit . . ." (219).

Ma expresses an intuitive sense of this welding when, in chapter 20, she says, "Why, Tom, we're the people that live. They ain't gonna wipe us out. Why, we're the people—we go on" (310). And a few paragraphs later, in an interchapter illustrating Ma's words, Steinbeck describes the migrant colonies as if the evicted sharecroppers had become one of the colonial sea creatures or schools with a single controlling drive: "The moving, questing people were migrants now. . . . The movement changed them. . . . And the hostility changed them, welded them, united them—hostility that made the little towns group and arm as though to repel an invader . . . (311–12). Like the colonial animals Steinbeck and Ricketts describe in the *Log,* the migrant families have joined together out of necessity. They have become a phalanx driving toward a single goal: group survival.

Finally even Ma, who has fought throughout the novel to keep the remnants of the family together, admits to Tom, "There ain't no family now" (434). Near the novel's end, stranded by rising flood waters in a boxcar camp, the remaining Joads merge with another family, the Wainwrights, whose daughter Al Joad plans to marry, and Steinbeck writes: "Now, without the separation, the two families in the car were one" (480). As the novel approaches its final tableau, Ma tells Mrs. Wainright, "Use' ta be the fambly was fust. It ain't so now. It's anybody" (491). And when, in the final scene, Ma silently encourages Rose of Sharon to nurse the dying man, this commitment to mankind as a whole is underscored.

Rose of Sharon's seemingly abrupt conversion from a self-centered, whining nuisance to a sympathetic Madonna-like character, in the novel's final chapter, has disturbed some critics who find insufficient motivation for her change. If we look rather closely at Rose of Sharon's relationship with Ma throughout the novel, however, it becomes evident that the daughter is the mother's disciple and has learned much from Ma. Just as Tom is growing throughout the novel toward his role as Casy's replacement, Rose of Sharon is moving steadily closer to Ma's selfless commitment to the larger whole. In the final three chapters of the novel, despite Ma's constant counseling, Rose of Sharon—following the most profound biological drive toward survival of the species—thinks only of the child she is carrying, framing every action and thought around the welfare of the new life. Even at the moment when the family is coming to terms with Tom's murder of the vigilante who has killed Casy, Rose of Sharon can think only of her child, crying hysterically, "An' now you kill a fella. What chance that baby got to get bore right?" (435) As noted above, evidence of a significant change in Rose of Sharon's character first becomes apparent, however, immediately after this scene when Tom awakens to find her standing beside him. "What you want?" he demands, with appropriate caution. Her response is "You sleep. . . . I'll watch the door. They won't nobody get in" (435–37). Until this point in the novel Rose of Sharon has felt responsible for only one thing, the life she has taken from the old place to the new.

Like the land turtle with its oat seed, Rose of Sharon has picked up life and carried it the length of the highway, and she feels an all-encompassing responsibility for the transplanting of that new life in the new homeland. Her intense, unthinking selfishness has been not for herself but for the progeny she nurtures, for the life of the people.

Rose of Sharon's full conversion to a different sense of responsibility comes about only near the novel's conclusion, however, and it is a new awareness stimulated by the impending marriage of her brother Al to the Wainwrights' daughter Aggie. As the flood waters prepare to inundate the stranded migrants, Rose of Sharon climbs into the boxcar shared by the two families and notices the excitement. "What's the matter?" she asks, and Ma replies, "Why, it's news! . . . We're going to have a little party 'count a Al an' Aggie Wainwright is gonna get married." Rose of Sharon's reaction is significant: "Rose of Sharon stood perfectly still. She looked slowly at Al, who stood there flustered and embarrassed." Then she goes away to contemplate what she has learned:

> Rose of Sharon turned slowly. She went back to the wide door, and she crept down the cat-walk. Once on the ground, she moved

slowly toward the stream and the trail that went beside it. *She took the way Ma had gone earlier*—into the willows. The wind blew more steadily now, and the bushes whished steadily. Rose of Sharon went down on her knees and crawled deep into the brush. The berry vines cut her face and pulled at her hair, but she didn't mind. Only when she felt the bushes touching her all over did she stop. She stretched out on her back. And she felt the weight of the baby inside of her. (469; my italics)

At this point Rose of Sharon is able to accept what unconsciously she must have known already: her baby is dead, it is simply a weight. In the impending marriage of Al and Aggie, however, she has become aware for the first time that the responsibility for ensuring that life goes on is not hers alone. The life she has carried has weighed heavily upon her, and at last she is able to acknowledge the weight of that responsibility while simultaneously awakening to the fact that all share equally the burden of life.

Aggie, whose name is linked unmistakably with the agricultural fecundity of the new land, is another incipient earth mother, just as the capable Al—who is handy with machines—will carry the family's life into new generations. Rose of Sharon is freed from individual responsibility and awakened to a sense of her place in the larger unit or group, the community of man. The wind that blows "more steadily" symbolizes this change in Rose of Sharon, just as the wind that blows as Tom declares his commitment to mankind symbolizes the change both in Tom Joad and in the conditions surrounding all of them. "On'y the wind, Ma," Tom had said. "I know the wind" (462).

When Rose of Sharon comes back from her symbolic rebirth in the womb-like cave of vines, she declares her intention to pick cotton to help the family. Ma Joad, who throughout the novel has groomed Rose of Sharon in her own image, intuits the change in her daughter. "What you wanta pick cotton for?" she asks, and then immediately she understands: " 'Is it 'cause of Al an' Aggie?' This time Ma looked closely at her daughter. 'Oh. Well you don' need to pick' " (471). Ma's "Oh" contains a world of meaning. Rose of Sharon now shares Ma's larger commitment: the people go on, and the individual's responsibility is to that whole, to what Steinbeck terms "Manself." When, in the novel's final scene, with Ma's encouragement, Rose of Sharon nurses the dying stranger, she is demonstrating this commitment by nurturing not a continuation of her individual self but a representative of humanity, of the species.

In this final scene all of the novel's philosophical and thematic threads come together. The book began with the prose rhythms and images of Exodus, and now the biblical flood seems to be rising over the corruption of California in a promise of a new beginning. The final lines of the penultimate chapter connect the rains with a faint but unmistakable hope for that new life: "Tiny points of grass came through the earth, and in a few days the hills were pale green with the beginning year" (480). The biblical symbolism in the novel has moved from Old Testament Exodus to a New Testament Christ (in Casy, Tom, and Rose of Sharon), culminating ironically in an Old Testament flood. The biological drive toward group survival—what in the *Log* was termed "group man" and in *The Grapes of Wrath* Steinbeck called "Manself," and what Casy described in transcendental terms echoing Emerson's Oversoul—has welded the people into larger units with a sense of responsibility not just to the individual or nuclear family but to all of life.

The frequent criticisms of the novel's conclusion indicate that critics have not generally understood the full import of Steinbeck's central theme. Representative of such dissatisfaction is one critic's declaration: "But if we consider the conclusion in relation to the total context of the novel, we see it as a thin veneer of affirmation concealing a logical and inexorable movement toward tragedy or pathos. Intended as positive upbeat, the episode only illustrates the more forcibly Steinbeck's inability to see where his novel came out, thematically."[61]

Rather than being a "thin veneer of affirmation," the conclusion strikes to the heart not just of the Joads' predicament but of the self-image of the nation as a whole. In the offering of Rose of Sharon's breast to the dying man, a tableau that recalls a popular image of the Madonna from Renaissance paintings, the biological, transcendental, and Christian threads of the novel come together. The theme of commitment to the larger whole, the essence of Christ's sacrifice, is illuminated in this giving of herself to a stranger, and the entire novel moves unwaveringly toward this final understanding: the isolated individual or the isolated family are no longer sufficient; we must be committed to all men and to "the whole thing."

Too much cannot be made of Rose of Sharon's rather unusual name. That Rose of Sharon's name is drawn from the Bible's Song of Solomon associates her firmly with Christ: "I am the rose of Sharon, and the lily of the valleys" (Song of Sol. 2.1). That whatever Promised Land exists has being only in man's commitment to man is suggested in another line from the same biblical text: ". . . thy stature is like to a palm tree, and they breasts to clusters of grapes" (7.7). The grapes, which have symbolized California and the new Canaan throughout the novel, are clearly associated with Rose of Sharon's offering of her breast to the old man here at the novel's end. Still another suggestion is called forth here, for the Song of Solomon is a celebration of life: "The flowers appear on the earth; the time of the singing of birds is come, and the voice of the turtle is heard in our land. . . ." (2.12). The Bible's use of the word "turtle" in place of turtledove for this song of life may account for the fact that Steinbeck chose to call the turtle of chapter 3 a "land turtle" rather than using the more appropriate term "tortoise." The land turtle prefigures the survival of the people just as Rose of Sharon's final gesture confirms that survival. Finally, as the flood waters rise about the barn where the remaining Joads have taken refuge, it should be remembered that from the Song of Solomon come these lines of promise: "Many waters cannot quench love, neither can the floods drown it. . . ." (8.7).

That America had long been a nation of individuals without commitment to one another or, even more importantly, without commitment to the place they inhabit—the entire ecosystem—is very much on Steinbeck's mind in this novel. It is this pattern of disengagement, Steinbeck suggests rather subtly, that has created the westering impulse, that movement which allows for the plundering of the continent in a steady westward migration. It is a historical pattern that pits man against man, family against family in a search for paradise. The sharecroppers, such as the Joads, who are quick to steal another man's home and guard it against recovery, and who readily embrace a history of killing Indians, are firmly fixed in this destructive pattern. What they must learn in the course of the novel is what Casy, Ma, Tom, and finally Rose of Sharon realize at last: it is through a Christ-like commitment to life itself that humanity will be sustained. What is essential is not the dubious survival of the individual Joads, but the migrants' new understanding and new commitment to the larger whole. Steinbeck stressed this point in a letter to Pascal Covici, his close friend and editor at Viking Press, who also had doubts about the ending:

> I am sorry but I cannot change that ending. It is casual. . . . if there is a symbol, it is a survival symbol not a love symbol, it must be an accident, it must be a stranger, and it must be quick. . . . The fact that the Joads don't know him, don't care about him, have no ties to him—that is the emphasis. The giving of the breast has no more sentiment than the giving of a piece of bread. . . . There are no new stories and I wouldn't like them if there were. The incident of the earth mother feeding by the breast is older than literature.[62]

That Rose of Sharon has discovered a deep sense of belonging to much more than herself or her family is suggested when Steinbeck writes: "For a minute Rose of Sharon sat still in the whispering barn. Then she hoisted her tired body up and drew the comfort about her" (501). Steinbeck's use of the word "comfort" to describe the kind of blanket most often called a "comforter" draws attention to the fact that in making her decision to feed the starving man Rose of Sharon has drawn about her the comfort of commitment to the larger whole. Her final smile, the novel's last act, suggests the fulfillment found in her new sense of place in the human community.

Steinbeck's easy movement from biology to Bible in this novel, that philosophical transition from colonial animal—mass man—to spiritual communion—Manself—argues convincingly against one of the most severe criticisms of this novel. Noting what he termed Steinbeck's "preoccupation with biology" in *The Grapes of Wrath* and elsewhere, esteemed critic and man of letters Edmund Wilson declared that "Mr. Steinbeck almost always in his fiction is dealing with human beings so rudimentary that they are almost on the animal level. . . . This animalizing tendency of Mr. Steinbeck's is, I believe, at the bottom of his relative unsuccess at representing human beings."[63] Disturbed, as were other critics, by Steinbeck's apparent naturalism, Wilson failed to recognize the deeply humanistic message of Steinbeck's writing.

Fundamental to Steinbeck's fiction is the author's acute awareness of biological man—man's inseparable oneness with the natural world. In *The Log from the Sea of Cortez* Steinbeck and Ricketts underscore this profound interpenetration of man and environment:

> We have thought often of this mass of sea-memory, or sea-thought, which lives deep in the mind. If one asks for a description of the unconscious, even the answer-symbol will usually be in terms of a dark water into which the light descends only a short distance. And we have thought how the human fetus has, at one stage of its development, vestigial gill-slits. If the gills are a component of the developing human, it is not unreasonable to suppose a parallel or concurrent mind or psyche development. If there be a life-memory strong enough to leave its symbol in vestigial gills, the preponderantly aquatic symbols in the individual unconscious might well be indications of a group psyche-memory which is the foundation of the whole unconscious. . . . The harvest of symbols in our minds seems to have been planted in the soft rich soil of our prehumanity. Symbol, the serpent, the sea, and the moon might well be only the signal light that the psycho-physiologic warp exists.[64]

If Steinbeck celebrates man's biological self and the deep imprint of our "prehumanity," however, he celebrates equally that spiritual and philosophical self which defines man's humanity and sets him apart from nature. "Carbon is not a man," Steinbeck writes in chapter 11 of *The Grapes of Wrath,* "nor salt nor water nor calcium. He is all these, but he is much more, much more . . ." (126). And, a few chapters later, in the novel's most ringingly idealistic prose, he adds:

> For man, unlike any other thing organic or inorganic in the universe, grows beyond his work, walks up the stairs of his concepts, emerges ahead of his accomplishments. This you may say of man—

when theories change and crash, when schools, philosophies, when narrow dark alleys of thought, national, religious, economic, grow and disintegrate, man reaches, stumbles forward, painfully, mistakenly sometimes. Having stepped forward, he may slip back, but only half a step, never the full step back. . . . fear the time when Manself will not suffer and die for a concept, for this one quality is the foundation of Manself, and this one quality is man, distinctive in the universe. (164)

In Rose of Sharon's final gesture, a Christ- and Madonna-like offering of the self, not for personal gain or even for a loved one, but simply for anonymous mankind, the step is taken which, in Steinbeck's words, defines man as "distinctive in the universe." The naturalistic Joads, who hunger and lust and follow biological urges with the best of animals, learn about themselves in the course of the novel. They take the crucial steps forward that Steinbeck describes in the interchapter. In the end Rose of Sharon has earned her biblical name, Al Joad has assumed a leadership role in place of his faltering father, and Tom has committed himself to suffering and possibly dying for a concept. In the process, Steinbeck has created characters both convincingly animal and inspiringly human.

10

Turtle and Truck: Animal, Machine, and Controlling Consciousness

While moving toward a level of almost mystical, intuitive knowledge near the novel's end, on a less profound level Steinbeck keeps the reader constantly aware of the biological nature of his characters through repeated animal associations. As Robert J. Griffin and William A. Freedman pointed out nearly a quarter of a century ago, "animal tropes abound" in the novel, as do animals themselves.[65] The most famous symbolic animal in the novel, of course, is the land turtle. Similarly, the ant lion trap (discussed in chapter 4) serves as a naturalistic symbol of the tenant farmers' plight. Once on the road, the terrors of the highway and the vulnerability of the migrants are underscored by the fate of the Joads' dog, which lacks the land turtle's good fortune:

> The dog wandered, sniffing, past the truck, trotted to the puddle under the hose again and lapped at the muddy water. And then he moved away, nose down and ears hanging. He sniffed his way among the dusty weeds beside the road, to the edge of the pavement. He raised his head and looked across, and then started over. Rose of Sharon screamed shrilly. A big swift car whisked near, tires squealed. The dog dodged helplessly, and with a shriek, cut off in

the middle, went under the wheels. The big car slowed for a moment and faces looked back, then it gathered greater speed and disappeared. And the dog, a blot of blood and tangled, burst intestines, kicked slowly in the road. (141)

Here, the ruthless force of machine America, the power which has tractored the migrants off their cropped-out land and with which they must contend once they reach California, hurtles past, seeming to gather speed from the power of its destructiveness. Later in the novel, the tenuous conditions of the migrants will again be suggested in the nervous mongrel that greets the Joads when they arrive in their first "Hooverville."

Throughout the novel, animals and animal tropes permeate nearly every paragraph, from "Muley" Graves to "Purty Boy Floyd" who, as Ma says, was run down "like a coyote." On the most obvious level, this proliferation of figures of speech involving animals is inevitable. Steinbeck is writing about a farming people, characters who live with animals and earn their livelihoods with animals. It is realistic that people whose lives are so deeply intertwined with the lives of animals would fashion metaphors around what they know so well. To create believable characters, Steinbeck must make them speak in this way. Mark Twain undoubtedly came to the same realization as he began to form Huckleberry Finn in his imagination. It is Huck Finn who gives us one of the most memorable descriptions in literature when he tells us that his Pa's face was "a tree-toad white, a fish-belly white." Like Steinbeck's migrants, Huck was drawing upon what he knew to fashion his metaphors.

The animal figures also, of course, serve to intensify our awareness of the biological nature of Steinbeck's characters. The migrants are not idealized abstractions. Like the Joads' dog, they are made of blood and intestines and driven by urges they do not begin to comprehend, such as Al's concupiscence and Uncle John's alcohol-abetted remorse. That the characters in the novel accept their own biological natures is evident in the families' attitudes toward the relationship between Al and Aggie. Expressing his concern for the growing intimacy between his daughter and Al Joad, Mr. Wainwright tells the Joads, "Well, her an' your boy Al, they're a-walking out ever' night. An' Aggie's a good healthy girl that oughta have a husban', else she might git in trouble." Ma's response is "Well, Al's a good boy. Kinda figgers he's a dung-hill rooster these days, but he's a good steady boy" (466). Neither parent passes moral judgment on the inevitable. Natural human / animal drives are accepted easily, as Wainwright indicates when he says simply, "It ain't Aggie's fault. She's growed up" (466). Care must simply be taken that such unavoidable biological urges do not cause awkward complications: both families look toward marriage as the appropriate step.

Steinbeck further illuminates the delicate line between man and his natural environment in his description of the abandoned sharecroppers' houses at the beginning of the novel:

> The doors of the empty houses swung open, and drifted back and forth in the wind. Bands of little boys came out from the towns to break the windows and to pick over the debris. . . . When the folks first left, and the evening of the first day came, the hunting cats slouched in from the fields and mewed on the porch. And when no one came out, the cats crept through the open doors and walked mewing through the empty rooms. And then they went back to the fields and were wild cats from then on, hunting gophers and field mice, and sleeping in ditches in the daytime. When the night came, the bats, which had stopped at the doors for fear of light, swooped into the houses and sailed about through the empty rooms, and in a little while they stayed in dark room corners during the day. . . . And the mice moved in and stored weed seeds in corners. . . . And weasels came in to hunt the mice, and the brown owls flew shrieking in and out. . . . (126)

In a single additional paragraph, Steinbeck goes on to depict in lyrical prose the disintegration of the house before the almost delicate onslaught of nature: rain, weeds, dust, wind. Beginning with the boys who come to break windows, regenerative nature reclaims the houses. Man's habitation is inhabited by the animal world; man's domesticated animals return to the wild with impressive ease and, like the migrants themselves, sleep in ditches. The boundary between man and nature seems infinitely permeable, transitory, illusory.

While the migrants are identified closely with the natural world, the mechanistic world stands in antithesis to the biological migrants. *The Grapes of Wrath* indeed abounds with examples of destructive machines, beginning with the light truck that swerves in order to hit the land turtle making its way across the highway. Later, not only will a car hit and kill the Joads' dog, but we will hear a story of a "Big Cad,'" which hit a truckful of migrants, killing one of the migrant children and throwing "bed clothes an' chickens an' kids" all around.

Epitomizing the destructive, depersonalizing machine is the tractor, which drives the sharecroppers from their land:

> The tractors came over the roads and into the fields, great crawlers moving like insects, having the incredible strength of insects. . . . Snubnosed monsters, raising the dust and sticking their snouts into it, straight down the country, across the country, through fences, through dooryards, in and out of gullies in straight lines. . . .
>
> The man sitting in the iron seat did not look like a man; gloved, goggled, rubber dust mask over nose and mouth, he was a part of the monster, a robot in the seat. . . .
>
> Behind the harrows, the long seeders—twelve curved iron penes erected in the foundry, orgasms set by gears, raping methodically, raping without passion. . . .
>
> The land bore under iron, and under iron gradually died; for it was not loved or hated, it had no prayers or curses. (36–38)

It is not the machine, however, that is evil but the uses to which it is put. "Is a tractor bad?" an interchapter voice asks. "Is the power that turns the long furrows wrong?" The answer is "If this tractor were ours it would be good—not mine, but ours. If our tractor turned the long furrows of our land, it would be good. . . . We could love that tractor then as we have loved this land when it was ours" (165).

Man, whose biological nature—epitomized by his sexuality—often seems uncontrollable in the novel, is capable of asserting control over machinery. The truck that has swerved to hit the turtle has simply forwarded the turtle's movement in the desired direction, flipping it like a tiddlywink, while Tom Joad's first act in the novel is to appropriate the power of the "huge red transport" with its "No Riders" sticker and make it transport him homeward. Despite the confusion of the used car lots, Al Joad is able to purchase a sound car for the family, convert it into a truck and nurse the vehicle all the way to California. Man can develop an almost mystical feeling for machinery as he can for the land, Steinbeck suggests. "Funny how you fellas can fix a car," Casy tells Tom. And Tom responds: "Got to grow into her when you're a little kid. . . . It ain't jus' knowin'. It's more'n that. Kids now can tear down a car 'thout even thinkin' about it" (203).

In spite of the repeated threat of destructive machines in the novel, man is capable of asserting a humanistic order amidst the mechanized chaos. Man's genius has created the abundance of California's orchards and fields. "And men are proud," Steinbeck writes, "for of their knowledge they can make the year heavy. They have transformed the world with their knowledge" (474). Scientific or mechanical genius alone, however, is insufficient: "Men who have created new fruits in the world cannot create a system whereby their fruits may be eaten. And the failure hangs over the State like a great sorrow" (385). It is man's responsibility and, Steinbeck declares, man's ability to control the machinery of that agricultural system for the benefit of humanity. Steinbeck underscores this responsibility in a declaration worth quoting once again: "For man, unlike any other thing organic or inorganic in the universe, grows beyond his work, walks up the stairs of his concepts, emerges ahead of his accomplishments" (164).

11

Beyond Blame or Cause:
The Nonteleological Joads

In 1940 Steinbeck and his marine biologist friend Edward F. Ricketts chartered a boat for a journey from Monterey, California, to the Gulf of California with the goal of collecting marine invertebrates in the Gulf. The following year Steinbeck and Ricketts published *Sea of Cortez*, co-authored from notes gathered during the trip, with no explicit evidence as to whose ideas were whose in the work. In 1951, three years after Ed Ricketts's death, Steinbeck published *The Log from the Sea of Cortez*, the narrative portion of the original book minus most of the scientific data. While the Gulf of California may seem a world away from the trials of the Dust Bowl refugees in *The Grapes of Wrath*, to understand Steinbeck's philosophy in this novel and, in particular, his attitudes toward the migrants we need to consult this narrative, written less than one year after the publication of Steinbeck's major novel. For *The Log from the Sea of Cortez* can shed invaluable light on Steinbeck's treatment of both the Joads and the entire Dust Bowl phenomenon.

The philosophical posture that Steinbeck and Ricketts called "non-teleological thinking" is of primary importance in its application to *The Grapes of Wrath*, as well as to much of Steinbeck's other fiction. Teleology is defined in the glossary to the *Log* as "The assumption of predetermined design, purpose, or ends in Nature by which an explanation of phenomena is postulated."[66] The *Log* further expounds upon this kind of thought: "What we personally conceive by the term "teleological thinking" . . . is most frequently associated with the evaluation of causes and effects, the purposiveness of events. . . . In their sometimes intolerant refusal to face the facts as they are, teleological notions may substitute a fierce but ineffectual attempt to change conditions which are assumed to be undesirable, in place of the understanding-acceptance which would pave the way for a more sensible attempt at any change which might still be indicated."[67] According to Steinbeck's and Ricketts's definition, "non-teleological thinking concerns itself not with what should be, or could be, or might be, but rather with what actually 'is.'"[68] Thus the desired nonteleological thinking may be defined as "is" thinking, or nonblaming thought. Steinbeck and Ricketts further qualify their definition of nonteleological thinking: "Strictly, the term non-teleological thinking ought not to be applied to what we have in mind. Because it involves more than thinking, that term is inadequate. Modus operandi might be better— a method of handling data of any sort. . . . The method extends beyond thinking even to living itself; in fact, by inferred definition it transcends the realm of thinking possibilities, it postulates 'living into.'"[69]

That Steinbeck was profoundly influenced by this way of viewing reality is abundantly evident in *To a God Unknown,* the novel the author drastically revised after meeting Ed Ricketts in 1930. In that novel the protagonist, Joseph Wayne, makes a fierce but ineffectual attempt to end a drought, which, in his limited vision, he thinks is destroying the land. All of Joseph Wayne's sacrifices and nature worship are fruitless, however, because nonteleologically the drought is simply something that "is," something that cannot be changed and must be accepted. Again, a few years later, in his first attempt in a novel to deal with migrant farm workers, *In Dubious Battle,* Steinbeck adopted a nonteleological or nonblaming posture. The strike by the workers is treated similarly to the drought in *To a God Unknown;*

it is a phenomenon that simply "is." While he illustrates the inhumanity and cruelty on both sides of the strike, Steinbeck's primary interest in the novel, as he defined it in a letter to a friend, is to be "merely a recording consciousness, judging nothing, simply putting down the thing."[70] The strike in that novel grows out of an unchanging quality in man's basic nature. "I have used a small strike in an orchard valley," Steinbeck wrote of the novel, "as the symbol of man's eternal, bitter warfare with himself."[71] In that novel Doc Burton becomes a spokesman for both Steinbeck's evolving thoughts concerning group man and the kind of nonteleological thinking defined in the *Log*.

And, still again, in his next novel, *Of Mice and Men* (1937), the novel immediately preceding *The Grapes of Wrath*, Steinbeck adopted a nonteleological posture. Originally entitled "Something that Happened," *Of Mice and Men* studies the phenomenon of Lenny, a huge man with the moral and intellectual development of an infant. The novel makes it clear that no one is really to blame for the seeming tragedy that befalls Lenny and George. Lenny is huge and dangerous, as his killing of virtually everything he touches makes clear. Like a drought, Lenny's flawed self is an accident of nature and something that cannot be helped, a fact accepted by George when he shoots Lenny at the novel's end. Although the various kindnesses and cruelties in the novel are obviously meant to draw a moral response from the reader, for the central catastrophe of Lenny Small no one is to blame; Lenny's misshapen mind is just something that happened.

In the space of four incredible years Steinbeck published what are probably his three finest novels: *In Dubious Battle*, *Of Mice and Men*, and *The Grapes of Wrath*. Each novel is a radically different kind of formal experiment and each focuses from a different perspective upon the conditions surrounding migrant farm laborers in California. Within these three novels we see an evolution in Steinbeck's thinking about the migrants and the farm labor situation in his home country. *In Dubious Battle* is a hard, objective and at times brutal look at the striking workers. While maintaining the nonteleological stance of the first novel, *Of Mice and Men* shifts perspective to examine closely and sympathetically an intimate friendship between two of the wandering workers. And *The Grapes of Wrath,* in its narrative chapters, moves closer yet to its subjects in a compassionate depiction of widespread suffering. There can be no doubt that as he learned more about the realities of the migrant laborers' plight Steinbeck became more deeply involved and sympathetic, as his newspaper pieces about the migrants' situation and his monograph, *Their Blood Is Strong,* make evident.

In spite of Steinbeck's increasing sympathy with the suffering of the migrants, however, *The Grapes of Wrath* demonstrates once again much of the same nonteleological thinking that governed the first two parts of this farm labor trilogy. On the one hand, Steinbeck makes it clear that on a short-term basis the disaster of the Dust Bowl can be traced to particular causes such as the excessive planting of cotton; similarly, the immediate cause of the tenants' eviction may be seen as the foreclosures by banks and the institution of large-scale tractor farming. But if we look at the bigger picture, it becomes evident that no one in particular is at fault. Dry years have made farming more difficult; no one is to blame for the weather. The sodbusters who stole the land from the Indians settled in a region not ideally suited to farming; recurrent droughts have made that clear. Repeated failures forced them to rely upon the banks for loans to keep going. Repeated plantings of cotton to pay off the interest on mortgages drained nutrients from the soil while both the cutting of trees to open up more farmland and the arrow-straight furrows of plows across the plains exposed the soil to the wasting winds. While mistakes have been made on a large, national and regional scale, no one individual is at fault here.

The farmers are caught up in a pattern of American expansion and settlement that is beyond their comprehension. The banks, like the tenant farmers, aim simply at survival; they must show a profit to survive, and to show a profit they must evict the small-acreage sharecropper. Together, the system tears the heart out of the land and makes it inhospitable to man.

That all of this has happened, and that the farmers lose their land and go on the road is, on one level, simply a fact, the way it "is." Just as we should not blame the ant lion for the fate of the ant in its trap, we can assign no direct blame for the tragedy of the migrants. To blame the farmers for improper agricultural methods would be point-less, just as it would be fruitless to blame the banks or the men who represent the banks. Such attempts to assign blame would distract from what was defined in the *Log* as "the understanding-acceptance which would pave the way for a more sensible attempt at any change which might still be indicated."[72] And the change that is indicated is on a very large scale; it is a change in the very way Americans think about the land and about themselves.

When the representative migrant voice says, in chapter 5, "We've got a bad thing made by men, and by God that's something we can change" (40), he is voicing precisely Steinbeck's posture as a social critic in this novel. What the cropper cannot see, however, is that the "bad thing made by men" goes far beyond the farmers' eviction from the land, beyond the banks' foreclosures, beyond tractor farming and profit-taking. The "bad thing" is a national consciousness, the product of several centuries of historical process. Of the impulse to assign blame for what goes wrong, the authors of the *Log* wrote: "One feels that one's neighbors are to be blamed for their hate or anger or fear. One thinks that poor pavements are 'caused' by politics. The non-teleological picture in either case is the larger one that goes beyond blame or cause. . . . The new viewpoint very frequently sheds light over a larger picture, providing a key which may unlock levels not accessible to either of the teleological viewpoints."[73]

Ma Joad is an accomplished nonteleological thinker, as Steinbeck demonstrates in Ma's encounter with the company store clerk at the Hooper Ranch. Confronted with the absurdly high prices of the com-pany store and the defensive belligerence of the clerk, Ma directs her anger for an instant at the man behind the counter before seeing be-yond to the larger picture:

> She looked up, smiling a little. "Ever'body comes in talks like me, is mad?"
> He hesitated for a moment, "Yes, ma'am."
> . . . "Doin' a dirty thing like this. Shames ya, don't it? Got to act flip, huh?" Her voice was gentle. The clerk watched her, fasci-nated. . . . "That's how it is," Ma said. (414)

Beyond Blame or Cause: The Nonteleological Joads

In *The Grapes of Wrath,* Steinbeck is attempting to shed light over the larger picture, to go beyond simply blaming the land owners, banks, or other immediate factors in order to "unlock" levels of insight into American culture, American history, and American thought. That the tenant farmers as well as others in the novel cannot see the larger picture, and that most of Steinbeck's readers failed to see the larger picture, is to be expected, for we are all caught up in the very process the novel attempts to illuminate. "Anything less than the whole forms part of the picture only," the authors of the *Log* wrote, "and the infinite whole is unknowable except by *being* it, by living into it."[74]

Besides Ma, whose steady wisdom lies in her nonteleological vision, one character who succeeds in going beyond the "partial indices" in order to see the whole picture is Jim Casy. By the time we encounter him for the first time, Casy has already had his time in the desert and has arrived at a rather incoherent, mystical, nonblaming and Christlike comprehension. It is Casy who most fully "lives into" an understanding of the larger picture, as is evidenced when he echoes Christ as he is about to be killed: "You fellas don' know what you're doin'." That Steinbeck and Ricketts in the *Log* make a connection between their definition of nonteleological thinking—the "living into" an intuitive sense of man's place in the larger picture—and Emerson's Oversoul underscores the often-noted parallel between Casy's mystical philosophy and Emersonian transcendentalism.

As Casy's disciple Tom Joad moves steadily toward his own sense of the "larger picture." Whereas he begins the novel as a quintessentially American individualist who says of himself "I'm just tryin' to get along without shovin' nobody around," by the end of the novel Tom has come to grasp Casy's sense of "one big soul," of commitment to the larger whole. "Well, maybe like Casy says," he tells Ma, "a fella ain't got a soul of his own, but on'y a piece of a big one . . . (463). Like Casy, Tom will commit himself to changing only those things that can be changed, and his goal is to change the way people think, to put an end to the celebrated individualism so inherent in the American self-image: "All work together for our own thing—all farm our own lan' " (463). Just as Henry David Thoreau had no difficulty reconciling

Emersonian transcendentalism with political activism, Tom and Casy have swung the Oversoul into the realm of labor action.

In the opening chapters of *The Grapes of Wrath*, it is clear that Steinbeck is not so much interested in assigning blame as he is in studying the phenomenon of the mass human movement. We may, like Grampa and Muley Graves, feel angry or disheartened that Willy Feeley or Joe Davis's boy chooses to earn his three dollars to support his family by helping to drive the other sharecroppers away, but the tractor driver, too, is caught up in a larger pattern. We may not like the representatives of the banks and corporations who come to speak to the croppers, but, as they correctly point out, the individuals are not at fault.

As the novel progresses and the Joads and the other migrants arrive in California, however, the authorial voice changes and becomes accusatory. In his preface to *The Forgotten Village*, Steinbeck had written, "We did not editorialize, attack, or defend anything. We put on film what we found. . . ."[75] In the interchapters of *The Grapes of Wrath*, the authorial voice achieves a freedom not allowed in the documentary film as, in the voice of an Old Testament prophet, Steinbeck denounces what is happening in California: "There is a crime here that goes beyond denunciation. There is a sorrow here that weeping cannot symbolize. There is a failure here that topples all our success. The fertile earth, the straight tree rows, the sturdy trunks, and the ripe fruit. And children dying of pellagra must die because a profit cannot be taken from an orange. . . . In the souls of the people the grapes of wrath are filling and growing heavy, growing heavy for the vintage" (385). While the drought, the blowing winds, even the shift from tenant farming to tractor farming are simply facts that must be accepted, man's inhumanity to man in the corrupt garden of California is a crime and is declared to be such. Unlike the drought and the immediate conditions in the region of the Dust Bowl, this is a condition that can, and as Steinbeck makes clear, will be changed. Similarly, the pattern of thought that led Americans to look always westward and away from commitment to the here and now, which ultimately, Steinbeck suggests, is responsible for the tragedy of the Dust Bowl, can and must be changed.

12

From Genesis to Jalopies: A Tapestry of Styles

Perhaps no aspect of Steinbeck's accomplishment in *The Grapes of Wrath* has been overlooked as often as the sheer genius of prose style throughout the novel. Peter Lisca brought this quality to our attention more than three decades ago when he declared that "No other American novel has succeeded in forging and making instrumental so many prose styles."[76] In spite of Lisca's observation, however, in critics' rush to evaluate such elements as the novel's unique structure, the Christian symbolism, and the political message, the brilliance of varied voices in the novel has been given short shrift.

The Grapes of Wrath does indeed bring together a complexity of narrative voices seldom equalled in American fiction, beginning with the epic voice of the novel's opening lines, with their quick blending of impressionistic image and matter-of-fact observation:

> To the red country and part of the gray country of Oklahoma, the last rains came gently, and they did not cut the scarred earth. The plows crossed and recrossed the rivulet marks. The last rains lifted the corn quickly and scattered weed colonies and grass along the sides of the roads so that the gray country and the dark red country began to disappear under a green cover. . . . The sun flared down

on the growing corn day after day until a line of brown spread along
the edge of each green bayonet. (1)

In addition to the structural and symbolic significance of this opening
paragraph, which is noted earlier in this study, these lines demonstrate
an immediate and impressive flexing of the narrative voice. From the
lyrical impressionism of the first line, which establishes the epic sweep
of the novel, the tone shifts rapidly but smoothly as the focus narrows.
It is the matter-of-fact voice of the naturalist that, beginning in the
second line, begins to document seemingly objective details of the
scene: plow marks, quick growth, weeds and grass, seared edge of
corn leaf. The precise dating underscores this blend of impression and
fact: "In the last part of May the sky grew pale . . ." (1).

Already the two major qualities of voice that will form the peculiar strength of this novel have been established: the lyrical, prophetic tone that will carry the burden of sympathetic humanism
throughout the novel; and the more objective, nonjudgmental tone
that will counterbalance the novel's intense sympathy for the migrants.
As one voice reports facts as they are, from a nonteleological posture,
the second voice enters the novel as judge and prophet. The voice of
the humanist begins by echoing the Bible, recalling throughout the
opening paragraphs the parallelism, simple conjunctions, and epic
sweep of the prophets. In the course of the novel this voice will grow
from the broad lyricism of Genesis, which is suggested in these opening paragraphs, to the harsh admonitory tone of the New Testament,
with which the interchapter voice warns: "There is a crime here that
goes beyond denunciation. There is a sorrow here that weeping cannot
symbolize. There is a failure here that topples all our success. . . . In
the souls of the people the grapes of wrath are filling and growing
heavy, growing heavy for the vintage" (385). The epic, biblical voice
is the voice of the interchapters where the enormity of the national
error is displayed and condemned. Dominating the style throughout
these chapters is the lyrical parallelism suggestive always of immensity
and scale. A quick glance at excerpts from the interchapters illustrates
the quality of voice that is peculiar to this part of the novel:

The houses were left vacant on the land, and the land was vacant because of this. Only the tractor sheds of corrugated iron, silver and gleaming, were alive; and they were alive with metal and gasoline and oil, the disks of the plows shining. The tractors had lights shining, for there is no day and night for a tractor and the disks turn the earth in the darkness and they glitter in the daylight. (125–26)

The moving, questing people were migrants now. Those families who had lived on a little piece of land, who had lived and died on forty acres, had eaten or starved on the produce of forty acres, had now the whole West to rove in. . . . And the companies, the banks worked at their own doom and they did not know it. The fields were fruitful, and starving men moved on the roads. The granaries were full and the children of the poor grew up rachitic, and the pustules of pellagra swelled on their sides. (311, 313)

Some of the owner men were kind because they hated what they had to do, and some of them were angry because they hated to be cruel, and some of them were cold because they had long ago found out that one could not be an owner unless one were cold. (32)

Countering the deeply accusatory and often morally outraged voice of the interchapters is the naturalistic, objective voice of the narrative chapters. In these chapters the Joads and those characters involved in the Joads' lives are described from the objective standpoint of the interested, at times even amused, but primarily non-judgmental observer, or are simply allowed to speak for themselves in their own voices. The shortcomings of these characters become obvious at once. Grampa is not only vicious, but "cruel and impatient, like a frantic child. He drank too much when he could get it, ate too much when it was there, talked too much all the time" (84). Granma "was as mean as her husband," with a "shrill ferocious religiosity that was as lecherous and as savage as anything Grampa could offer" (84). Uncle John wallows in the self-pity brought on by the death of his wife. Al wallows in concupiscence. Rose of Sharon is oblivious to any needs but her own. Connie, with his soft-minded belief in the futures promised in such aptly titled magazines as *Western Love Stories,* is a short step away from the tractor drivers who have deserted their people. Pa is so self-centered that Tom will tell Casy late in the novel, "Think Pa's gonna give up his meat on account a other fellas?" Tom has killed a man in a drunken brawl and says of women, "I never let nothin' go by when I could catch it" (23). Even Ma, the larger-than-life embodiment of female virtue in the novel, has beaten a pedlar brutally with a live chicken.

The matter-of-fact voice of the narrative chapters tells us these things without judging, or allows the characters themselves to inform us through speech and action. This is the nonteleological voice of the marine biologist who observes specimens in the tidepool. This is the way things are, the way people are, something to be accepted. And it is to a large degree this voice that prevents *The Grapes of Wrath* from slipping fatally into the kind of sentimental admiration for the working masses that damaged so many "proletarian" novels of the thirties.

Another, closely related counterpoint going on within the novel is that of the epic, biblical voice and the idiomatic voice of the people. Just as the narrative chapters and the interchapters move us alternately closer to and away from the Joads, suggesting two vital levels to this tragedy, the idiomatic folk-voice and the epic biblical voice move us between two levels: the American tragedy of the Dust Bowl, which is suggested by the recognizably American vernacular, and the broadly human level of misunderstanding that reaches beyond America, which is suggested by the biblical voice. On the one hand, the vernacular voice links the Joad chapters with the interchapters that focus on representative, faceless migrants. The identical voices tell us that the people of the interchapters are the faceless Joads and that the Joads, among many thousands of families that might have offered the same degree of suffering and selflessness, are simply one family under scrutiny. On the other hand, the epic voice of the interchapter, with its biblical style, suggests that more profound, universal failures lie beneath the immediate failure of the Dust Bowl.

Within the two powerful kinds of voices dominating the novel is an impressive array of other styles. One such style is that of the chanting, staccato voice of repetitive motion, the monosyllables in a hammering series of fragments, the facts from the map of America that move us with the force of pure motion:

> Highway 66 is the main migrant road. 66—the long concrete path across the country, waving gently up and down on the map, from the Mississippi to Bakersfield—over the red lands and the gray lands, twisting up into the mountains, crossing the Divide and down into the bright and terrible desert, and across the desert to the mountains again, and into the rich California valleys. . . .
>
> Clarksville and Ozark and Van Buren and Fort Smith on 64, and there's an end of Arkansas. And all the roads into Oklahoma City, 66 down from Tulsa, 270 up from McAlester. 81 from Wichita Falls south, from Enid north. Edmond, McLoud, Purcell. 66 out of Oklahoma City; El Reno and Clinton, going west on 66. Hydro, Elk City, and Texola; and there's an end to Oklahoma. 66 across the Panhandle of Texas. Shamrock and McLean, Conway and Amarillo, the yellow. Wildorado and Vega and Boise, and there's an end of Texas. Tucumcari and Santa Rosa and into the New Mexico mountains to Albuquerque, where the road comes down from Santa Fe. Then down the gorged Rio Grande to Las Lunas and west again on 66 to Gallup, and there's the border of New Mexico. (127–28)

Or, when Steinbeck wants the reader to share the confusion and chaos the sharecroppers experience in their first visit to a used car lot, he writes a cacophony of prose such as that in chapter 7:

> In the towns, on the edges of the towns, in the fields, in vacant lots, the used-car yards, the wreckers' yards, the garages with blazoned signs—Used Cars, Good Used Cars. Cheap transportation, three trailers. '27 Ford, clean. Checked cars, guaranteed cars. Free radio. Car with 100 gallons of gas free. Come in and look. Used Cars. No overhead. . . .
>
> Square noses, round noses, rusty noses, shovel noses, and the long curves of streamlines, and the flat surfaces before streamlining. . . . Cadillacs, La Salles, Buicks, Plymouths, Packards, Chevies, Fords, Pontiacs. Row on row, headlights glinting in the afternoon sun. Good Used Cars. (65–70)

In the clashing consonants and onrush of prose we feel the frightened, bewildered confusion of the farmers hoarding their last dollars toward two thousand miles of unknown highway.

When Steinbeck wants, on the other hand, to suggest the joy of lives caught up in delirious motion, the prose style metamorphoses into pure music, as it does in the square dance scene of chapter 23. Here, as the narrative voice describes the dance, we slip unconsciously into the rhythm of the square dance caller:

> Look at that Texas boy, long legs loose, taps four times for ever' damm step. Never seen a boy swing aroun' like that. Look at him swing that Cherokee girl, red in her cheeks an' her toe points out. Look at her pant, look at her heave. Think she's tired? Think she's winded? Well, she ain't. Texas boy got his hair in his eyes, mouth's wide open, can't get air, but he pats four times for ever' darn step, an' he'll keep a'goin' with the Cherokee girl.
>
> The fiddle squeaks and the guitar bongs. Mouth-organ man is red in the face. Texas boy and the Cherokee girl, pantin' like dogs an' a-beatin' the groun'. Ol' folks stan' a-pattin' their hans. Smilin' a little, tappin' their feet. (363–64)

Here, for a brief time the Joads have found security in the government camp at Weedpatch. The dance becomes a celebratory moment in the lives of the migrants and within the increasingly harsh events of the Joads' new life. For a moment the reader, too, is allowed to be swept into the pure joy of life. The brief passage is a small tour de force, an ingenious rendering in prose of the square dance rhythm in three brief paragraphs slipped incidentally into the vast sweep of the novel. The casual brilliance of the prose here is stunning.

At last, in the final interchapter the prophetic voice of the novel returns full circle back to the tone of the opening pages as once again the inexorable force of nature is brought to bear upon the people: "Over the high coast mountains and over the valleys the gray clouds marched in from the ocean. The wind blew fiercely and silently, high in the air, and it swished in the brush, and it roared in the forests. The clouds came in brokenly, in puffs, in folds, in gray crags; and they piled in together and settled low over the west. And then the wind stopped and left the clouds deep and solid" (477). Just as the biblical style of the first chapter with the compelling power of its parallelism and repetition suggests both the creative force of Genesis and the plagues God's wrath sent against Egypt, here that voice returns as a flood—of what seems to be biblical dimensions—begins to rise over the corrupted landscape of California. That this is a story of the "west"—much like Fitzgerald's *The Great Gatsby*—and therefore of America itself is emphasized by the scope of this storm that settles vaguely "over the west." In this prophetic voice, upon high ground amidst this flood, the novel will end with an affirmation of life.

13

From Oklahoma to Hollywood:
The Grapes of Wrath on Film

To suggest Steinbeck's success with film as well as with fiction, it is only necessary to list movies and television adaptations born from his novels or scripts: *The Grapes of Wrath, East of Eden, Of Mice and Men, Tortilla Flat, The Forgotten Village, The Moon Is Down, Lifeboat, A Medal for Benny, The Pearl, The Red Pony, Viva Zapata!, The Wayward Bus, Flight, Cannery Row,* and *The Winter of Our Discontent.* Television adaptations from *The Pastures of Heaven* alone include "Molly Morgan," "Nobody's Fool," "Nothing So Monstrous," and "The House." [77] No other American writer has seen his works move so easily and surely onto the screen. And with the possible exception of Lewis Milestone's brilliant adaptation of Steinbeck's play / novella *Of Mice and Men,* no Steinbeck work moved from page to screen so successfully as *The Grapes of Wrath.*

In 1939 Hollywood producer Darryl F. Zanuck paid Steinbeck $75,000 for film rights to the *The Grapes of Wrath.* According to Steinbeck biographer Jackson Benson, Steinbeck and Zanuck met just before the film was to go into production. The author, who had destroyed a draft of the novel because it was not "honest," and who had refused payment for writing about the desperate migrants, reportedly told the producer that he intended to put the $75,000 into an escrow account. If in the transition to the screen the novel was "watered down or its perspective changed," he would use the money to sue Zanuck. Zanuck, in turn, assured Steinbeck that he had hired a detective agency to check out the accuracy of the script and that the agents had found conditions much worse than Steinbeck had reported.[78]

Steinbeck was so concerned that his novel be left undiluted he suggested that 20th Century-Fox contact Tom Collins, administrator of the Weedpatch camp, and the man to whom the novel is dedicated, and arrange for Collins to act as advisor. Steinbeck wrote to Collins himself to say, "I think they are doing an honest job. . . . Don't go out on a limb until we see the script, but good people are working on it. My thought is that if they can get 10% on film it will be worthwhile.[79] To his agent, Elizabeth Otis, Steinbeck wrote: ". . . they [20th Century-Fox] sent a producer into the field with Tom Collins and he got sick at what he saw and they offered Tom a job as technical assistant which is swell because he'll howl his head off if they get out of hand."[80]

In the end, Tom Collins would receive prominent billing as the movie's "Technical Director" in the credits, and Steinbeck would be pleased with the script, written by Nunnally Johnson, and the film, produced by Zanuck and directed by John Ford. After seeing the movie, which cost $750,000 to make, Steinbeck wrote again to Otis:

> Zanuck has more than kept his word. He has a hard, straight picture in which the actors are submerged so completely that it looks and feels like a documentary film and certainly it has a hard, truthful ring. No punches were pulled—in fact, with descriptive matter removed, it is a harsher thing than the book, by far.
> . . . it opens sometime in January. There is so much hell being raised in this state that Zanuck will not release simultaneously. He'll open in N. Y. and move gradually west, letting the publicity precede it. . . . He has hired attorneys to fight any local censorship. . . . All this is far beyond our hopes.[81]

So much hell was indeed still being raised by the best-selling novel that when filming began along the migrant pathway across the West the film was shot under the title of "Route 66" to discourage hostility. Both Steinbeck's admiration for the "hard, straight picture" and his concern for potential controversy, however, are difficult to understand when we review the film today. Together, Zanuck and Ford succeeded in more than muting the political message of the novel and producing a film that—brilliant though it may be in many ways—turns Steinbeck's call for a rebirth of national consciousness into a sentimental celebration of the American "salt of the earth."[82]

With Steinbeck, Zanuck and Ford had a writer whose work made the transition from page to screen with astonishing ease. A large portion of credit for this ease must go to Steinbeck's own fascination with documentary filmmaking. While writing *The Grapes of Wrath,* Steinbeck had met documentary artist Pare Lorentz, whose credits included the classic *The Plow that Broke the Plains* as well as *The River.* With Lorentz, Steinbeck talked about film and even journeyed to Hollywood briefly.[83] Steinbeck's fascination with documentary film would deeply influence the tone and structure of *The Grapes of Wrath* and lead, two years later, to his own documentary film, *The Forgotten Village.*

From the opening lines of the first paragraph, *The Grapes of Wrath* is obviously a camera-conscious novel as the narrative eye zooms in and pans back from the devastated landscape. When Tom Joad appears in the novel, he is a solitary figure walking into focus in a setting already arranged for the camera: a little roadside restaurant, a huge red transport truck with a muttering smokestack outside, a road running past through dusted-out farmland. Steinbeck's almost invariable technique of firmly fixing his setting before bringing on his characters lends itself perfectly to both drama and film, and the detached, nonjudgmental (nonteleological) tone fits neatly the detached interest of the documentary camera. The episodic nature of Steinbeck's fiction, particularly in *The Grapes of Wrath,* also fits neatly into the scenic structure of most films.

That Steinbeck was documenting a current phenomenon made Zanuck and Ford's task still easier: all the producer and director had to do to envision their characters and scenes was to look at the Dust

Bowl and depression photographs by people like Dorothea Lange and Horace Bristol. Bristol, who had accompanied Steinbeck into the fields as a photographer for *Life* magazine, would say in a 1987 article for the *San Francisco Chronicle*, "It is no coincidence that several of the principal characters in the movie *The Grapes of Wrath* resemble my photographs, for the 20th Century Fox directors asked me for a set to help them cast for the movie." In the same article, which reprinted the photographs Bristol took for *Life*, the photographer suggested that his pictures "might serve to remind a new generation of readers that Steinbeck's characters were not figments of his imagination but living, breathing, suffering Americans."[84]

The Grapes of Wrath was an immense success on the screen, 20th Century-Fox's top money-maker of the year, selected as best picture of 1940 by the National Board of Review and the New York Film Critics, and winner of Academy Awards for Ford (best director) and Jane Darwell (best supporting actress in the role of Ma). Reviewers raved and audiences flocked to see it. The *New York Times* declared the film to be "just about as good as any picture has a right to be."[85]

While it would be absurd to judge the success of a movie according to its faithfulness to the novel it sprang from, Zanuck and Ford's *The Grapes of Wrath* offers interesting insights into Steinbeck's book. Both Nunnally Johnson, in writing his script for the film, and John Ford, in directing the movie, were confronted with the obvious problem of the novel's bulk. Just as obvious as the need to reduce the dimensions of Steinbeck's story must have been the logical choice of which of the brief interchapters to omit. Although elements of the interchapters were eventually incorporated into the film, particularly in the few panoramic shots, the ultimate effect of such condensing was to focus exclusively on the Joads rather than Steinbeck's "Manself."

Ford, whose earlier credits included the great movie *Stagecoach*, attempted to establish a sense of historical context by inserting two paragraphs of prose on the screen immediately following the opening credits: "In the central part of the United States of America lies a limited area called 'the Dust Bowl,' because of its lack of rains. Here drought and poverty combined to deprive many farmers of their land.

This is the story of one farmer's family, driven from their fields by natural disasters and economic changes beyond anyone's control and their great journey in search of peace, security, and another home." One interesting effect of seeing this prose up on the screen may be to link, at least subliminally, movie to novel—film to written word—and to remind the reader of the best-selling source of what he is about to experience.

Other effects are more interesting yet. Immediately, in its description of "a limited area called 'the Dust Bowl,' " the prose serves to limit the scope of the tragedy about to be witnessed to a specific, isolated part of the nation. The suggestion that this area is called thusly "because of its lack of rain" gives an impression of a somewhat timeless quality of that region. The simple past tense used in the final sentence of the first paragraph underscores a feeling that it is all over by the time of the film, 1940. The second paragraph prepares us not for Steinbeck's picture of failure on a national scale but for the story of "one farmer's family," who are victims of changes "beyond anyone's control," and who will set out on a heart-rending journey "in search of peace, security, and another home."

While the prose here certainly emphasizes Steinbeck's own non-teleological message that no one individual is to blame for what is happening to the migrants, the message is slanted, a forewarning of the director's attempt to carefully avoid attaching specific blame in this potentially controversial film. As wanderers in search of "peace" and "security," the Joads are introduced in very unthreatening roles. The possibility of social change wrought by violent conflict suggested in the novel will not even be hinted at in the movie.

Dispensing with the broad panorama of landscape and human distress with which the novel begins, the movie commences with an opening shot of a small, distant silhouette of a man approaching a stark crossroad. Overhead, telephone poles and black lines of crossing wires emphasize the image of the crossroad. When the walking man approaches the "Cross Road" café, Ford's point is complete: the man will turn out to be Tom Joad, just out of prison and about to reach a crossroad in his life. It is a brilliant beginning and one Steinbeck would surely have found in harmony with the intentions of his novel. Moments later, in a scene right out of the novel, Tom kicks up dust as he walks toward his meeting with Casy.

In one of the movie's finest scenes, the image of the cross reappears in the window of the abandoned Joad house, very obvious against the gathering storm outside. And the nonteleological message of Steinbeck's novel is picked up again in this scene when, in a flashback, we see Muley Graves being evicted from his farm. Told by the spokesman for the big corporate owners that there is no one individual or group of individuals to blame, Muley asks, "Then who do we shoot?" The spokesman, sitting in his sleek automobile, replies, "Brother, I don't know." It should be remembered, however, that Steinbeck does in fact assign blame in his novel. What is happening is the fault not of individuals or groups specifically; it is the fault of a system originating in a mind-set, an idea the nation has developed about itself over centuries.

In the novel this mind-set is evoked in the form of the American myth and the pattern of American settlement when the migrant voice cries out "Grampa killed Indians, Pa killed snakes for the land." In the movie, however, this reminder of collective guilt—along with the novel's depiction of the migrants' willingness to barter war and death for a chance to hang on—is omitted, and the more innocuous words of the faceless migrant from chapter 5 of the novel are incorporated into Muley's speech: "My grampa took up this land seventy years ago. My pa was born here. We was all born on it." In one of the finest scenes in the movie, John Qualen, as Muley, concludes: "And some of us died on it. That's what makes it our'n."

While here it is neither necessary nor possible to make comparisons between novel and movie scene by scene, what becomes apparent at once in these opening scenes, and will remain apparent throughout the movie, is a shift between fiction and film from the group ("Manself") to the heroic individual. *The Grapes of Wrath* as a novel argues that in order to survive spiritually and physically on the planet man must commit himself to man and environment, to "the whole thing, known and unknowable." *The Grapes of Wrath* as film focuses upon the traditional figure of the isolated individual—as the opening shot of Tom Joad indicates—who will, without challenging the frontier mentality upon which the nation is founded, make things "right." The single accordion playing the homely folk tune "Red River Valley" in the background at strategic moments throughout the movie under-scores this muted longing for an earlier time when the heroic individual could wrest livelihood and security from the land. This message—fundamentally one of Jeffersonian agrarianism—is absolutely opposed to the message of Steinbeck's novel, though it is a proven winner with American audiences.

A major structural shift between novel and film occurs when Ford inverts the order of the Hooper Ranch (Keene Ranch in the movie) and Weedpatch camp episodes, change that drastically alters Stein-beck's story. In the novel, the family is forced to leave the government camp where they have experienced security and respect for the first time on their journey. From the orderly camp they go to the peach orchards of the strike-bound Hooper Ranch. There, Casy is murdered, Tom kills Casy's murderer, and the family flees to the boxcar camp where they will make their penultimate stand for survival. From the temporary idyll of the Weedpatch government camp, the Joads' fortunes arc despairingly downward in an unbroken line toward the final scene in the barn. Things for the migrants go from bad to worse, to say the least.

Dissatisfied with such a grim conclusion, the movie's creators take the Joads from the Dantesque hell of the peach ranch to the bucolic haven of the Weedpatch camp. In the movie, the camp director (in real life, Tom Collins) is a saintly fellow with a decided resemblance to a beardless Santa Claus. The episode features the lyrical interlude of the dance, interrupted briefly by the skirmishers, and also the saccharine scene in which Ruthie and Winfield discover indoor plumbing. Finally, Tom suspects that he is about to be discovered and he sets off on his own.

The movie ends with the Joads leaving the scecurity of the camp, but the tone is upbeat all the way. "I don't know what you folks are hurry'n so for," someone in the camp tells the departing family. "They tell me there's twenty days work up there." Pa responds: "Yes sir, and we aim to get in all twenty of 'em." The message seems to be that a positive work ethic is the answer to the migrants' problems.

As the truck jolts along, Al beams: "Twenty days work! Oh, Boy!" and Ma says, "Mebbe. Mebbe twenty days work and mebbe no days work. We ain't got it till we get it." Following this necessary dose of realism, however, Ma says, "For a while it looked as though we was beat. Good and beat. Looked like we didn't have nobody in the whole wide world but enemies. . . . Like we was lost and nobody cared." Pa adds, ". . . we shore taken a beatin'," and Ma responds with an incongruous chuckle and the final speech of the movie as "Red River Valley" strikes up in the background: "I know. That's what makes us tough. Rich fellas come up an' they die, an' their kids ain't no good, an' they die out. But we keep a-comin'. We're the people that live. They can't wipe us out. They can't lick us. We'll go on forever, Pa, 'cause we're the people." As Warren French has pointed out, the implications of this final speech are that "there will always be rich and poor, aristocrats and peasants, but that the aristocrats will rise, dissipate themselves and disappear, while the peasants will keep trudging down a long, hard road.[86] There is no sense of impending revolt, of smouldering injustice, nothing, in short, to make property owners insecure. We are left with admiration for these durable, heroic, but humble people who seek only the right to labor for their daily bread. The sense of impending change, enormous change, which swells toward the end of Steinbeck's novel, simply is not here.

The movie's final image brings Ford's creation full circle as a line of rattletrap vehicles trundles along the bottom of the screen. Above the migrant cars and trucks a post with a sign attached forms a subdued cross with a line of dawn's light crossing post and sign. "Red River Valley" plays from a single accordion in the background.

According to one source, Zanuck himself was responsible for the sentimental ending: "Originally, in the end, Tom Joad leaves his family to become a labor organizer and activist, to do something not only for the Joads but all oppressed workers. Zanuck wanted something tidier, and he wrote a speech for Ma Joad. . . . Ford explains the inclusion [of Ma's speech]: 'This picture ended on a down note, and the way Zanuck changed it, it came out on an upbeat.' "[87] Regardless of who actually penned and inserted Ma's speech and decreed this particular ending for the movie, it is clear that producer and director worked to tone down Steinbeck's novel. An example that will stand for innumerable dilutions and omissions is the question of communism. In the novel, Tom has a chance to work briefly digging a ditch. During a pause, he asks a fellow worker, "What the hell is these reds anyways?" The answer, delivered in a somewhat lengthy vignette, is "A red is any son-of-a-bitch that wants thirty cents an hour when we're payin' twenty-five." "Hell . . . we're all reds," the character in the vignette exclaims (329). In the movie, during the scene in question Tom asks, "What is these reds anyway?" and there is no answer. Instead, the question dangles impotently for an instant before the subject is changed.

By ending the movie as he did Ford avoided the rather downbeat problem of Rose of Sharon's stillborn baby; the baby is as yet unborn and we know no more than that. And he did not have to come to terms with Steinbeck's controversial conclusion: Rose of Sharon's breast-feeding of the dying stranger. Thus the movie ends without the destructive, cleansing flood, without the symbolic stillbirth, and without the final gesture of universal love. The tottering line of little cars, the serene strength of Ma's words and face, and the dawning day all point toward not change but survival. The audience leaves one of the most powerful of American films moved and comforted, but not, as Steinbeck must have wished, provoked.

The brilliance of Ford's directing—uneven editing notwithstanding—combined with perhaps the finest casting in any Hollywood film (with the exception of the unbearably well-fed and irrepressible children) and the superb camera work of photography director Gregg Toland resulted in a movie that certainly deserves to be called a masterpiece. To state, as Life magazine did in 1940, however, that the movie "makes no compromises" and that "Bitter, authentic, honest, it marches straight to its tragic end. . . . with a courage that merits a badge of honor for the United States movie industry"[88] is to miss the obvious. Rather than marching straight to a tragic end, the film rounds slowly toward sentiment.

Principal Cast for *The Grapes of Wrath*

Tom	Henry Fonda
Ma	Jane Darwell
Pa	Russell Simpson
Grampa	Charley Grapewin
Granma	Zeffie Tilbury
Uncle John	Frank Darien
Noah	Frank Sully
Al	O. Z. Whitehead
Rose of Sharon	Dorris Bowdon
Connie Rivers	Eddie Quillan
Ruthie	Shirley Mills
Winfield	Darryl Hickman
Casy	John Carradine
Muley Graves	John Qualen

NOTES

1. Quoted in Jackson J. Benson, *The True Adventures of John Steinbeck, Writer* (New York: Viking Press, 1984), 291.

2. *Steinbeck: A Life in Letters*, ed. Elaine Steinbeck and Robert Wallsten (New York: Viking Press, 1975), 98.

3. *A Life in Letters*, 132.

4. Benson, *True Adventures*, 336.

5. Ibid., 336.

6. Ibid., 337.

7. *A Life in Letters*, 158.

8. Ibid., 159.

9. Carey McWilliams, "California Pastoral," in *The Grapes of Wrath: Text and Criticism*, ed. Peter Lisca (New York: Penguin Books, 1977), 657.

10. Ibid., 162.

11. Steinbeck, "A Letter on Criticism," in *Steinbeck and His Critics: A Record of Twenty-Five Years*, ed. E. W. Tedlock, Jr., and C. V. Wicker (Albuquerque: University of New Mexico Press, 1957), 52.

12. Benson, *True Adventures*, 376.

13. *A Life in Letters*, 178.

14. Martin Staples Shockley, "The Reception of *The Grapes of Wrath* in Oklahoma," in *Steinbeck and His Critics*, 233.

15. Shockley, "The Reception of *The Grapes of Wrath* in Oklahoma," in *Steinbeck and His Critics*, 237-38.

16. Joseph Henry Jackson, "The Finest Book John Steinbeck Has Written," in *A Companion to The Grapes of Wrath*, ed. Warren French (New York: Viking Press, 1963), 115.

17. Malcolm Cowley, quoted in "Editor's Introduction: The Pattern of Criticism," *The Grapes of Wrath: Text and Criticism*, 696.

18. Edmund Wilson, quoted in "Editor's Introduction: The Pattern of Criticism," *The Grapes of Wrath: Text and Criticism*, 696.

Notes

19. Joseph Warren Beach, "John Steinbeck: Art and Propaganda," in *Steinbeck and His Critics*, 250.

20. Ibid., 264.

21. Harry Thornton Moore, in "Editor's Introduction: The Pattern of Criticism," *The Grapes of Wrath: Text and Criticism*, 696.

22. Maxwell Geismar, *Writers in Crisis: The American Novel 1925-1940* (New York: Hill & Wang, 1947), 263–64.

23. Woodburn O. Ross, "John Steinbeck: Naturalism's Priest," in *Steinbeck and His Critics*, 214.

24. Frederick I. Carpenter, "The Philosophical Joads," in *Steinbeck and His Critics*, 242.

25. Bernard Bowron, "*The Grapes of Wrath*: A 'Wagons West' Romance," in *A Companion to The Grapes of Wrath*, 208–216.

26. Martin Staples Shockley, "Christian Symbolism in *The Grapes of Wrath*," in *Steinbeck and His Critics*, 266–71.

27. Eric W. Carlson, "Symbolism in *The Grapes of Wrath*," in *The Grapes of Wrath: Text and Criticism*, 749.

28. Walter F. Taylor, "*The Grapes of Wrath* Reconsidered," in *The Grapes of Wrath: Text and Criticism*, 765.

29. J. Paul Hunter, "Steinbeck's Wine of Affirmation in *The Grapes of Wrath*" in *Twentieth Century Interpretations of The Grapes of Wrath*, ed. Robert Con Davis (Englewood Cliffs, N. J.: Prentice-Hall, 1982), 47.

30. Agnes McNeill Donohue, " 'The Endless Journey to No End': Journey and Eden Symbolism in Hawthorne and Steinbeck," in *A Casebook on The Grapes of Wrath*, ed. Agnes McNeill Donohue (New York: Thomas Y. Crowell, 1968), 264–65.

31. Robert J. Griffin and William A. Freedman, "Machines and Animals: Pervasive Motifs in *The Grapes of Wrath*," in *The Grapes of Wrath: Text and Criticism*, 769-83. Betty Perez, "House and Home: Thematic symbols in *The Grapes of Wrath*," in *The Grapes of Wrath: Text and Criticism*, 840–53. Paul McCarthy, "House and Shelter as Symbol in *The Grapes of Wrath*" *South Dakota Review* (1967):48–67.

32. Warren French, "John Steinbeck and Modernism," in *Steinbeck's Prophetic Vision of America*, ed. Tetsumaro Hayashi and Kenneth D. Swan, Proceedings of the Bicentennial Steinbeck Seminar, 1 May 1976 (Upland, Ind.: Taylor University, 1976), 51.

33. See, for example, Joan Hendrick, "Mother Earth and Earth Mother: The Recasting of Myth in Steinbeck's *The Grapes of Wrath*, *Twentieth Century Interpretations of The Grapes of Wrath*, 134–43; Patrick W. Shaw, "Tom's Other Trip: Psycho-Physical Questing in *The Grapes of Wrath*," *Steinbeck Quarterly* 16, nos. 1–2 (Winter–Spring 1983):17–25; Helen Lojek, "Jim Casy: Politico of the New Jerusalem," *Steinbeck Quarterly* 15, no. 1–2

(Winter-Spring 1982):30–37; Richard S. Pressman, " 'Them's Horses—We're Men': Social Tendency and Counter-Tendency in *The Grapes of Wrath*," *Steinbeck Quarterly* 19, nos. 3–4 (Summer–Fall 1986):71–79.

34. R. W. B. Lewis, "John Steinbeck: The Fitful Daemon," in *Steinbeck: A Collection of Critical Esssays*, ed. Robert Murray Davis (Englewood Cliffs, N. J.: Prentice-Hall, 1972), 163, 173.

35. Malcolm Cowley, quoted in "Editor's Introduction: The Pattern of Criticism," in *The Grapes of Wrath: Text and Criticism*, 696.

36. *A Life in Letters*, 178–79.

37. John Steinbeck, *The Log from the Sea of Cortez* (New York: Viking Press, 1951), 217.

38. Steinbeck, *The Forgotten Village* (New York: Viking Press, 1941), 5.

39. Peter Lisca, *John Steinbeck: Nature and Myth* (New York: Thomas Y. Crowell, 1978), 106–7.

40. *A Life in Letters*, 171.

41. For discussions of the Christian symbolism see in particular Peter Lisca, *John Steinbeck: Nature and Myth*, 106–110; Martin S. Shockley, "Christian Symbolism in *The Grapes of Wrath*," in *Steinbeck and His Critics*, 266–71; and Joseph Fontenrose, *John Steinbeck: An Introduction and Interpretation* (New York: Holt, Rinehart & Winston, 1963), 75–83.

42. *The Log from the Sea of Cortez*, 218.

43. William Bradford, *Of Plymouth Plantation*, ed. Harvey Wish (New York: Capricorn Books, 1962), 36.

44. Edward Johnson, *Johnson's Wonder-Working Providence*, ed. J. Franklin Jameson (New York: Barnes & Noble, 1959), 30.

45. Steinbeck, *Journal of a Novel* (New York: Viking Press, 1969), 39.

46. Chester E. Eisenger, "Jeffersonian Agrarianism in *The Grapes of Wrath*," in *The Grapes of Wrath: Text and Criticism*, 723.

47. Ibid., 722.

48. Ibid., 725.

49. Ibid., 728.

50. Edmund Wilson, *The Boys in the Back Room: Notes on California Novelists* (San Francisco: Colt Press, 1941), 61.

51. Bernard De Voto, "American Novels: 1939," *Atlantic Monthly* 165 (January 1940):68.

52. R. W. B. Lewis, "John Steinbeck: The Fitful Daemon," *Steinbeck: A Collection of Critical Essays*, 171.

53. *The Log from the Sea of Cortez*, 75.

54. *East of Eden* (New York: Viking Press, 1952), 6.

55. Ibid., 35.

Notes

56. *A Life in Letters*, 80.

57. *In Dubious Battle* (New York: Viking Press, 1936), 131.

58. *A Life in Letters*, 76.

59. *The Log from the Sea of Cortez*, 167–68.

60. Ibid., 243.

61. Stuart L. Burns, "The Turtle or the Gopher: Another Look at the Ending of *The Grapes of Wrath*," *Twentieth Century Interpretations of The Grapes of Wrath*, 104.

62. *A Life in Letters*, 178.

63. Edmund Wilson, *Classics and Commercials: A Literary Chronicle of the Forties* (New York: Farrar, Straus & Co., 1950), 42.

64. *The Log from the Sea of Cortez*, 32–33.

65. Griffin and Freedman, "Machines and Animals: Pervasive Motifs in *The Grapes of Wrath*" in *The Grapes of Wrath: Text and Criticism*, 771.

66. *The Log from the Sea of Cortez*, 275.

67. Ibid., 138–39.

68. Ibid., 135.

69. Ibid., 150.

70. *A Life in Letters*, 98.

71. Ibid.

72. *The Log from the Sea of Cortez*, 138.

73. Ibid., 151.

74. Ibid., 151–52.

75. *The Forgotten Village*, 5.

76. Peter Lisca, "*The Grapes of Wrath* as Fiction," in *The Grapes of Wrath: Text and Criticism*, 742.

77. Joseph R. Millichap, *Steinbeck and Film* (New York: Frederick Ungar, 1983), 163–66.

78. Benson, *True Adventures*, 409.

79. Ibid., 410.

80. *A Life in Letters*, 186.

81. Ibid., 195.

82. Warren French has written perceptively on the relationship between the novel and film in his *Filmguide to The Grapes of Wrath* (Bloomington: Indiana University Press, 1973). I am indebted to his excellent research and analysis here.

83. Benson, *True Adventures*, 372.

84. Horace Bristol, "Steinbeck's Faces: The Real People Behind His Characters," *San Francisco Chronicle*, "This World," 25 Oct 1987, 13.

85. French, *Filmguide to The Grapes of Wrath*, 59.

86. French, *Filmguide to The Grapes of Wrath*, 37.

87. Mel Gussow, *Don't Say Yes Until I Finish Talking* (Garden City, N. Y.: Doubleday, 1971), 86. Quoted in French, *Filmguide*, 31. French disputes Zanuck's authorship of Ma's final speech.

88. Ibid., 59.

SELECTED BIBLIOGRAPHY

Primary Sources

Novels

The Grapes of Wrath is widely available in paperback through Penguin Books, the edition used in this study. The most useful edition for students is Peter Lisca's *The Grapes of Wrath: Text and Criticism*. New York: Viking Press, 1972.

The Acts of King Arthur and His Noble Knights. Chase Horton, editor. New York: Farrar, Straus & Giroux, 1976.

Burning Bright. New York: Viking Press, 1950.

Cannery Row. New York: Viking Press, 1945.

Cup of Gold: A Life of Henry Morgan, Buccaneer, with Occasional References to History. New York: Robert M. McBride, 1929.

East of Eden. New York: Viking Press, 1952.

The Grapes of Wrath. New York: Viking Press, 1939.

In Dubious Battle. New York: Covici-Freide, 1936.

Journal of a Novel: The East of Eden Letters. New York: Viking Press, 1969.

The Long Valley. New York: Viking Press, 1938.

The Moon is Down. New York: Viking Press, 1942.

Of Mice and Men. New York: Covici-Freide, 1937.

The Pastures of Heaven. New York: Brewer, Warren & Putnam, 1932.

The Pearl. New York: Viking Press, 1947.

The Red Pony. New York: Covici-Freide, 1937.

The Short Reign of Pippin IV: A Fabrication. New York: Viking Press, 1957.

Sweet Thursday. New York: Viking Press, 1954.

To A God Unknown. New York: Robert O. Ballou, 1933.

Tortilla Flat. New York: Covici-Freide, 1935.

The Wayward Bus. New York: Viking Press, 1947.
The Winter of Our Discontent. New York: Viking Press, 1961.

Nonfiction

America and Americans. New York: Viking Press, 1966.
The Log from the Sea of Cortez. New York: Viking Press, 1951. The narrative portion of *Sea of Cortez: A Leisurely Journal of Travel and Research,* 1941. With preface "About Ed Ricketts."
Once There Was a War. New York: Viking Press, 1958.
A Russian Journal. New York: Viking Press, 1948.
Steinbeck: A Life in Letters. Edited by Elaine Steinbeck and Robert Wallsten. New York: Viking Press, 1975.
Their Blood Is Strong. San Francisco: Simon J. Lubin Society of California, 1938.
Travels with Charley in Search of America. New York: Viking Press, 1962.
Vanderbilt Clinic. New York: Presbyterian Hospital, 1947.

Secondary Sources

Bibliographies

Beyer, Preston. "The *Joad Newsletter.*" *Steinbeck Quarterly* 4 (Fall 1971):105–106.

DeMott, Robert. *Steinbeck's Reading: A Catalogue of Books Owned and Borrowed.* New York: Garland, 1984.

Gross, John, and Lee Richard Hayman. *John Steinbeck: A Guide to the Collection of the Salinas Public Library.* Salinas, Calif.: Salinas Public Library, 1979.

Hayashi, Tetsumaro. *A Handbook for Steinbeck Collectors, Librarians, and Scholars.* Steinbeck Monograph Series, no. 11. Muncie, Ind.: Steinbeck Society, Ball State University, 1981.

———. *A New Steinbeck Bibliography: 1929–1971.* Metuchen, N. J.: Scarecrow Press, 1973.

———. *A New Steinbeck Bibliography: 1971–1981.* Metuchen, N. J.: Scarecrow Press, 1983.

Selected Bibliography

Woodress, James. "John Steinbeck" in *American Fiction, 1900–1950: A Guide to Information Sources*. Detroit: Gale Research Co., 1974, 183–93.

Biographies

Benson, Jackson. *The True Adventures of John Steinbeck, Writer*. New York: Viking Press, 1984.

Kiernan, Thomas. *The Intricate Music: A Biography of John Steinbeck*. Boston: Little, Brown, 1979.

Valjean, Nelson. *John Steinbeck: The Errant Knight: An Intimate Biography of His California Years*. San Francisco: Chronicle Books, 1975.

Book-Length Critical Studies and Collections

Astro, Richard. *John Steinbeck and Edward F. Ricketts: The Shaping of a Novelist*. Minneapolis: University of Minnesota Press, 1973. A study of the relationship between Steinbeck and marine biologist Ed Ricketts and its influence on Steinbeck's fiction.

———, and Tetsumaro Hayashi, editors. *Steinbeck: The Man and His Work*. Corvallis: Oregon State University Press, 1971. Critical essays discussing such works as *Viva Zapata!*, *In Dubious Battle*, *Cannery Row*, and *Sweet Thursday*, as well as Steinbeck's philosophy and the Steinbeck hero. Including "John Steinbeck: A Reminiscence," by Steinbeck's lifelong friend, Webster Street.

Davis, Robert Con, editor. *Twentieth Century Interpretations of the Grapes of Wrath: A Collection of Critical Essays*. Englewood Cliffs, N. J.: Prentice-Hall, 1982. Standard criticism of *The Grapes of Wrath*, including such major essays as Warren French's "From Naturalism to the Drama of Consciousness—The Education of the Heart in *The Grapes of Wrath*" and Peter Lisca's "*The Grapes of Wrath*: An Achievement of Genius." Newer essays consider the novel's intercalary chapters as well as Ma Joad as archetype.

Davis, Robert Murray, editor. *Steinbeck: A Collection of Critical Essays*. Englewood Cliffs, N. J.: Prentice-Hall, 1972. Twelve essays on such varied works as *Tortilla Flat*, *Of Mice and Men*, *In Dubious Battle*, *The Red Pony*, *The Grapes of Wrath*, *The Log From the Sea of Cortez*, *Cannery Row*, and *The Pearl*, with an introduction by Davis and a negative overview of Steinbeck's career by R. W. B. Lewis.

Ditsky, John, editor. *Critical Essays on The Grapes of Wrath*. Boston: G. K. Hall, 1989. Contains several original essays on *The Grapes of Wrath* stressing new approaches to the novel.

Ferrell, Keith. *John Steinbeck: The Voice of the Land* New York: M. Evans & Co., 1986. Critical overview of the author's life and work written with younger readers in mind.

French, Warren, editor. *A Companion to "The Grapes of Wrath."* New York: Viking Press, 1963. Groundwork collection of essays organized according to "Background," "Reception," and "Reputation" of the novel, including Steinbeck's monograph on migrant worker conditions, *Their Blood Is Strong*.

————. *The Social Novel at the End of An Era.* Carbondale: Southern Illinois University Press, 1966. A close look at the social context of the thirties, with extensive analysis of *The Grapes of Wrath*.

————. *A Filmguide to The Grapes of Wrath.* Bloomington: Indiana University Press, 1973. Monograph-length discussion of the direction and production of John Ford's film version of the novel, with scene-by-scene analysis, summary critique, bibliography, and novel-screenplay-film comparison.

————. *John Steinbeck, Revised Edition.* Boston: Twayne, 1975. Extensively revised version of the 1961 critical overview of Steinbeck's major fiction and nonfiction, published in Twayne's United States Authors Series.

Geismar, Maxwell. *Writers in Crisis: The American Novel 1925–1940.* New York: Hill & Wang, 1947. Critical study of pre–World War II "proletarian" fiction, including *The Grapes of Wrath*.

Hayashi, Tetsumaro, editor. *A Study Guide to Steinbeck: A Handbook to His Major Works.* Metuchen, N. J.: Scarecrow Press, 1974.

————, editor. *John Steinbeck: A Dictionary of His Fictional Characters.* Metuchen, N. J.: Scarecrow Press, 1976. Description of characters and roles in Steinbeck's fiction.

————, editor. *Steinbeck's Literary Dimension: A Guide to Comparative Studies.* Metuchen, N. J.: Scarecrow Press, 1972. Includes essays comparing Steinbeck and such writers as William Faulkner, Ernest Hemingway, Émile Zola, and others, as well as survey of criticism and bibliography.

————, editor. *Steinbeck's Women: Essays in Criticism.* Steinbeck Monograph Series, no 9. Muncie, Ind.: Steinbeck Society, Ball State University, 1979. Essays discussing female characters in Steinbeck's fiction, including *The Grapes of Wrath*.

Levant, Howard. *The Novels of John Steinbeck: A Critical Study.* Columbia: University of Missouri Press, 1974. With an introduction by Warren French, a study focusing on theme and structure in Steinbeck's novels.

Lisca, Peter. *John Steinbeck: Nature and Myth.* New York: Crowell, 1978. A critical overview and introduction to Steinbeck's fiction.

————. *The Wide World of John Steinbeck.* New Brunswick, N. J.: Rutgers

University Press, 1958. Reprint. New York: Gordian Press, 1981. A more detailed study than *Nature and Myth*; thorough background research.

McCarthy, Paul. *John Steinbeck*. Modern Literary Monograph Series. New York: Ungar, 1980. A critical overview of Steinbeck's life and fiction.

Millichap, Joseph R. *Steinbeck and Film*. New York: Frederick Ungar, 1983. A study of the interrelationships between Steinbeck's films and his fiction, including *The Grapes of Wrath*.

Owens, Louis. *John Steinbeck's Re-Vision of America*. Athens: University of Georgia Press, 1985. A critical overview of major fiction with emphasis upon the American myth.

Tedlock, E. W., and C. V. Wicker. *Steinbeck and His Critics: A Record of Twenty-Five Years*. Albuquerque: University of New Mexico Press, 1957. A collection of twenty-nine essays and notes, including responses by Steinbeck to his critics.

Timmerman, John H. *John Steinbeck's Fiction: The Aesthetics of the Road Taken* (Norman: University of Oklahoma Press, 1986). The most recent critical overview of Steinbeck's major fiction.

Watt, F. *Steinbeck*. New York: Grove Press, 1962. Reprint. New York: Chips, 1978. Pioneering introductory critical study of Steinbeck's fiction.

Articles

Astro, Richard. "From the Tidepool to the Stars: Steinbeck's Sense of Place." *Steinbeck Quarterly* 10 (Winter 1977):5–11.

———. "John Steinbeck and the Tragic Miracle of Consciousness." *San Jose Studies* 1 (November 1975): 61–72.

Benson, Jackson J. "Environment as Meaning: John Steinbeck and the Great Central Valley." *Steinbeck Quarterly* 10 (Winter 1977):12–20.

———. "Through a Political Glass Darkly: The Example of John Steinbeck." *Studies in American Fiction* 12 (Spring 1984):45–59.

——— and Anne Loftis. "John Steinbeck and Farm Labor Unionization: The Backgrounds of *In Dubious Battle*." *American Literature* 52 (May 1980):194–223.

Benton, Robert M. "A Scientific Point of View in Steinbeck's Fiction." *Steinbeck Quarterly* 7 (Summer–Fall 1974):67–73.

Brasch, James D. "*The Grapes of Wrath* and Old Testament Skepticism." *San Jose Studies* 3 (May 1977):16–27.

Bredahl, A. Carl, Jr. "The Drinking Metaphor in *The Grapes of Wrath*." *Steinbeck Quarterly* 6 (Fall 1973):95–98.

Campbell, A. M. "Reports from Weedpatch, California; the Records of the Farm Security Administration." *Agricultural History* 48 (July 1974):402–4.

Carr, Duane R. "Steinbeck's Blakean Vision in *The Grapes of Wrath.*" *Steinbeck Quarterly* 8 (Summer–Fall 1975):67–73.

Cook, Sylvia. "Steinbeck, the People, and the Party." *Steinbeck Quarterly* 15 (Winter-Spring 1982):11–23.

Covici, Pascal, Jr. "Steinbeck's Quest for Magnanimity." *Steinbeck Quarterly* 10 (Summer–Fall 1977):79–89.

Cox, Martha Heasley. "The Conclusion of *The Grapes of Wrath*: Steinbeck's Conception and Execution." *San Jose Studies* 1 (November 1975):73–81.

———. "Fact into Fiction in *The Grapes of Wrath*: The Weedpatch and Arvin Camps." *John Steinbeck: East and West.* Steinbeck Monograph Series, no. 8. Edited by Tetsumaro Hayashi. Muncie, Ind.: Steinbeck Society, Ball State University, 1978,12–21.

DeMott, Robert. "The Interior Distances of John Steinbeck." *Steinbeck Quarterly* 12 (Summer–Fall 1979):86–99.

Ditsky, John. " 'Directionality': The Compass in the Heart." *The Westerning Experience in American Literature.* edited by M. Lewis and L. L. Lee (Bellingham, Wash.: Western Washington University, 1977). 215–20.

———. "The Ending of *The Grapes of Wrath.*" *Agora* 2 (Fall 1973):41–50.

———. "*The Grapes of Wrath*: A Reconsideration." *Southern Humanities Review* 13 (Summer 1979):215–20.

Fossey, W. Richard. "The End of the Western Dream: *The Grapes of Wrath* and Oklahoma." *Cimarron Review* 22 (1973):25–34.

French, Warren. "After *The Grapes of Wrath.*" *Steinbeck Quarterly* 8 (Summer–Fall 1975):73–78.

———. "The California Quality of Steinbeck's Best Fiction." *San Jose Studies* 1 (November 1975):9–19.

Gladstein, Mimi Reisel. "Ma Joad and Pilar: Significantly Similar." *Steinbeck Quarterly* 14 (Summer–Fall 1981):93–104.

Hayashi, Tetsumaro. "Steinbeck's Women in *The Grapes of Wrath*: A New Perspective." *Kyushu American Literature* 18 (October 1977):1–4.

Lewis, Clifford L. "Critical Perspectives on John Steinbeck's Fiction." *American Examiner* 6 (Fall–Winter 1978–79):69–86.

———. "*The Grapes of Wrath*: The Psychological Transition from Clan to Community." *American Examiner* 6 (Fall–Winter 1978–79):40–68.

———. "Jungian Psychology and the Artistic Design of John Steinbeck." *Steinbeck Quarterly* 10 (Summer–Fall 1977):89–97.

Lojek, Helen. "Jim Casy: Politico of the New Jerusalem." *Steinbeck Quarterly* 15 (Winter–Spring 1982):30–37.

Selected Bibliography

McCarthy, Paul. "House and Shelter as Symbol in *The Grapes of Wrath*." *South Dakota Review* 5 (1967–68):48–67.

Matto, Collin G. "Water Imagery and the Conclusion to *The Grapes of Wrath*." *NEMLA Newsletter* 2 (May 1970):44–47.

Pressman, Richard S. " 'Them's Horses—We're Men': Social Tendency and Counter-Tendency in *The Grapes of Wrath*." *Steinbeck Quarterly* 19 (Summer–Fall 1986):71–79.

Salter, Christopher L. "John Steinbeck's *The Grapes of Wrath* as a Primer for Cultural Geography." *Humanistic Geography and Literature: Essays on the Experience of Place*. edited by Douglas C. D. Pocock. London: Croom Helm, 1981, 142–58.

Shaw, Patrick W. "Tom's Other Trip: Psycho-Physical Questing in *The Grapes of Wrath*." *Steinbeck Quarterly* 16 (Winter–Spring 1983):17–25.

Slade, Leonard A., Jr. "The Use of Biblical Allusion in *The Grapes of Wrath*." *CLA Journal* 11 (March 1968):241–47.

Watkins, Floyd C. "Flat Wine from *The Grapes of Wrath*." *The Humanist in His World: Essays in Honor of Fielding*, edited by Barbara Bitter and Frederick Sanders. Greenwood, S. C.: Attic, 1976, 57–69.

INDEX

Index

ABOUT THE AUTHOR

Louis Owens is currently associate professor of English at the University of New Mexico. He is a member of the editorial board of the *Steinbeck Quarterly* and has published books and numerous essays on Steinbeck and other subjects. He has taught Steinbeck courses both in the United States and abroad as a Fulbright fellow at the University of Pisa, Italy. Owens's book-length study of Steinbeck's fiction, *John Steinbeck's Re-Vision of America*, was published in 1985, and in 1986 he was recognized as the Outstanding Teacher of the Year by the John Steinbeck Society of America.